SOCIAL SCIENCES & HISTORY

CLEP* Study Guide

All rights reserved. This Study Guide, Book and Flashcards are protected under the US Copyright Law. No part of this book or study guide or flashcards may be reproduced, distributed or stored in a retrieval system, or transmitted in any form or by any means, electronic, mechanical, photocopying, recording, or otherwise, without the prior written permission of the publisher Breely Crush Publishing, LLC.

© 2019 Breely Crush Publishing, LLC

*CLEP is a registered trademark of the College Entrance Examination Board which does not endorse this book.

971080818143

Copyright ©2003 - 2019, Breely Crush Publishing, LLC.

All rights reserved.

This Study Guide, Book and Flashcards are protected under the US Copyright Law. No part of this publication may be reproduced, distributed or stored in a retrieval system, or transmitted in any form or by any means, electronic, mechanical, photocopying, recording, or otherwise, without the prior written permission of the publisher Breely Crush Publishing, LLC.

Published by Breely Crush Publishing, LLC
10808 River Front Parkway
South Jordan, UT 84095
www.breelycrushpublishing.com

ISBN-10: 1-61433-545-1
ISBN-13: 978-1-61433-546-7

Printed and bound in the United States of America.

*CLEP is a registered trademark of the College Entrance Examination Board which does not endorse this book.

Table of Contents

United States History: Part I 1
    Columbus and the New World 1
    Establishing Colonies 1
    Life in the Colonies 2
    The Salem Witch Trials 2
    The Beginning of Slavery 3
    The Age of Enlightenment 3
    The Great Awakening 4
    Manifest Destiny 4
    Mercantile System 5
    Struggle for Independence 5
    Beginning of United States Democracy 6
    Alaska Purchase 8
    Slavery, Fight for Equality, Civil War and Reunification – 1850-1877 8
    The American Civil War 9
United States History: Part II 9
    Industrial and Infrastructural Growth 9
    World War I – The Most Powerful Nation 10
    Worldwide Depression and World War II 11
    The Cold War Era and Thereafter 13
    United States History – Points to Remember 17
Western Civilization 18
    Divine Right 18
    Ancient Western Asia, Greece and Rome 18
    Medieval History 22
    Medieval Europe 24
    Modern Europe 25
World History 28
    Africa 28
    Asia 29
    Australia 30
    North and South America 30
Government & Political Science 32
Sociology 37
    Ascribed and Achieved Status 39
    Research 39
    Socialchange, Social Organization, Social Stratification and Social Theory 41
    C. Wright Mills 42
    Frances Perkins 43

Economics *44*
    Keynesian Economics *44*
    Scarcity, Choice, Cost, Economics Measurement *45*
    Monetary and Fiscal Policy *46*
    Budget Deficits *47*
    International Trade *47*
Introduction to Psychology *49*
    Aggression *49*
    Conformity *50*
    Group Process Methods *51*
    Performance *51*
    Personality *51*
    Socialization *52*
    Memory *53*
    Agoraphobia *54*
    Ethnocentrism *54*
    Cultural Relativism *54*
Geography *55*
    Distance, Ecology, Location, Regional Geography, Spatial Interaction,
        Weather and Climate, Etc. *55*
    Great Lakes *58*
Introduction to Anthropology *59*
    Cultural Anthropology *59*
    Ethnography *60*
    Hominids *60*
Introduction to Religion *61*
    Buddhism *61*
    Judaism *61*
    Islam *62*
    Christianity *62*
    Taoism *63*
    Shamans *64*
    First Gothic Cathedral in France *64*
Sample Test Questions *65*
Test Taking Strategies *132*
What Your Score Means *132*
Test Preparation *133*
Legal Note *133*
References *133*

 United States History: Part I

COLUMBUS AND THE NEW WORLD

Native Americans have been living in North America for thousands of years. In the year 1492, Christopher Columbus, in trying to establish a sea-route to the Far East, fortuitously landed in a land mass subsequently called "The New World." This was one of the greatest discoveries in the history of the world. In the year 1519, Ferdinand Magellan started from Spain in ships, crossed the Atlantic and Pacific Oceans, and after making a complete circle of the world, one of his ships returned to Spain. This had proved beyond any reasonable doubt at that time that a separate continent – North America – existed between the two great oceans-the Atlantic and Pacific. The Europeans, French, English, Spanish, Dutch, and Swedes had shown interest in the New World. Jacques Cartier of France was also asked to find a short sea-route to the Far East. He, in the year 1534, explored along the St. Lawrence River and the French Government processed their claim on that part of North America.

Before the Age of Exploration changed perceptions of the world forever, spices were one of the most valuable commodities in the world. At the height of the spice trade some were even more valuable than gold. In fact, the search for spices is considered to be the quest that spurred on the Age of Exploration in Europe.

Most of the spices desired by Europeans were only to be found in South East Asia. This was a very long and difficult journey for European tradesman. In the 1400s, there was only one land route in existence. In addition to being treacherous at times, this route was heavily controlled by Muslim merchants seeking to make their own profits on the spice trade.

The high tariffs urged European rulers to spend great efforts in seeking another route to India. As a result, Christopher Columbus sailed across the ocean looking for an "Eastern Passage" and instead discovered the American continent. Frustrated by his failure to find passage to Asia, Columbus still called the native peoples "Indians." Others sailed around Africa, and Magellan circumnavigated the globe and it was all in a search for additional routes and access to spices.

ESTABLISHING COLONIES

The first English settlement was established on May 14, 1607 with a group of 105 colonists in Virginia and they called it Jamestown. Their main source of revenue was from growing and selling tobacco. The second English colony was established in December 21, 1620, with a group of more than 100 people in Plymouth (What is now known as Massachusetts). They came by a ship known as the "Mayflower." They adopted the "Mayflower Compact", which was the first attempt at self-government in the New World. 1623, New Hampshire became a settlement and in 1624 New York was developed by the Dutch and they called it New Netherlands.

In 1664, the English took control of New York from the Dutch. Then Maryland was settled in 1632. In 1636, Connecticut and Rhode Island were settled. Then North Carolina in 1653 and South Carolina in 1663 were settled. The last of the original 13 colonies was established by James Oglethorpe in the year 1733. There was in all 2,500,000 people in the 13 colonies in 1690. The colonies faced threat from the French, who were living in the St. Lawrence Valley, and the Mississippi Valley as well as the Great Lakes area. Constant fights over the fishing trade erupted between French and English settlers. There were many conflicts but the French and Indian began in 1754. In the year 1756 it spread to Europe. The French lost the war and the Treaty of Paris signed in 1783 brought to a halt war in the New World. The result was that Canada and all other French areas east of Mississippi came under English rule. Spain also gave Florida to the English – The supremacy of the English in the New World was firmly established and the English language prevailed.

LIFE IN THE COLONIES

The Northern colonies differed greatly from the Southern colonies. In fact, each colony was very different, with slightly different values and beliefs. The Northern colonies were formed around the church, literally. Each church was surrounded by houses and a "green" or "commons" where trade and other activities took place. The houses and colony life revolved around the church. Church and state were one in the Northern colonies.

In the Southern colonies, people were spread out on large plantations, far away from each other. The Southern colonies made their money from the plantations which took a lot of manpower to work. They had many indentured servants perform labor and eventually began purchasing slaves to help with the labor. Although many considered themselves religious, few went to church regularly and some people never attended. The colonists living in the Southern colonies imitated the rich in England and created their own social structures.

THE SALEM WITCH TRIALS

The Salem Witch Trials began when teenage girls began to accuse middle aged women of witchcraft. Because people were still superstitious at the time, this epidemic spread like wildfire. Over 300 women were convicted of witchcraft and more than 19 of them were executed with no proof.

Historians have since determined that the accusations arisen between two different social groups. Women who lived outside the norm of a woman's perceived role at the time (worked outside the home, etc.) were targeted.

THE BEGINNING OF SLAVERY

The Portuguese were the first to import black slaves into the New World. They began with sugar plantations and then moved many more into mining for gold and silver. Spain, England, Holland and France all participated in the buying and selling of slaves. The **Triangular Trade** was known as shipping lines that connected Europe, Africa and the America's with slaves. Slaves were also forced to endure a "seasoning" process where they were prepared for sale. About 30% of slaves died during this seasoning process.

All colonies had legalized slavery by 1750. Rising wages for indentured servants made slaves popular. Colonies developed laws to keep slaves under control. They restricted slaves of:

- Right to assembly
- Earning money
- Seek after an education
- Autonomy of movement

Many unspeakable acts were legal to perform on slaves under certain circumstances. The white colonists feared a slave revolt. Their livelihood depended on the willing or unwilling work of their slaves. Two slave revolts, one in South Carolina and one in New York, made slave owners more anxious than ever before.

THE AGE OF ENLIGHTENMENT

The Enlightenment was an intellectual movement in Europe starting in the 1700s. The predominant message of the Enlightenment was a movement from traditional and antiquated beliefs of the past to a search for knowledge and improvement in the future. The early stages of the Enlightenment were characterized by great improvements and discoveries in the fields of mathematics and science. The later stages were characterized by philosophical advances. The pursuit of knowledge led to everything from the creation of the first encyclopedias to the theories that formed a basis for the United States Constitution.

One of the most well-known figures of the late Enlightenment period was Voltaire. Born Francois-Marie Arouet, Voltaire was a sharp critic of Catholic dogmas and French institutions that prohibited progression. Although he was imprisoned several times throughout his life, he continued to write countless articles, plays, and scientific works.

His commitment to social reform and freedom of expression earned him the respect of being known as one France's greatest writers and philosophers.

This was the beginning seeds of the American Dream, that all people can excel and succeed if they work hard. This was a far cry from the caste system that someone was born into. In the caste system, if you were born to a fisherman, you would be a fisherman or other tradesman and marry the children of the same. Very rarely did people cross classes, marrying up or down. Status could not be changed easily.

John Locke created an idea called **Theory of Contract under Natural Law**. The idea was the kings, queens, princes, etc., were not divinely determined by God but instead were just born lucky. He believed that all people had natural rights to life, liberty and happiness. Locke had a great influence on the people, in fact, much of his ideas appeared in the Declaration of Independence when he wrote that everyone had a right to "life, liberty and the pursuit of happiness."

THE GREAT AWAKENING

The Great Awakening, 1730s, was a time when religion, which had been put on the back burner, became very prominent and important again. Many important preachers contributed to this new excitement for religion.

George Whitefield was a young 27 year old man who preached to thousands of people at a time. He believed that the people lacked passion because "dead men preach to them." Whitefield created dramas and skits about the pleasures of heaven and the pains of hell. He used entertainment to draw and keep his congregations.

Jonathan Edwards did not use entertainment to draw his congregation. He talked of fire and brimstone, trying to scare his flock into choosing what was right. One of his sermons "Sinners in the Hands of an Angry God" is one of the most famous sermons in American history.

The Great Awakening did more than get the colonists into church. It also stimulated an interest in reading and spurred the distribution of books and the creation of schools and libraries. The Great Awakening was the beginning of the separation of church and state.

MANIFEST DESTINY

Colonists believed that America was destined to grow and colonize west. This was thought of as a divine right and stewardship.

MERCANTILE SYSTEM

Spain, England, France, Portugal and other European countries believed in a mercantile system. Power was linked to wealth and wealth was linked to trade. Each country encouraged their manufacturing plants to create as many goods as possible and tried to protect their own industries. England forbade the colonies to ship their good anywhere but England, so a tax could be added before items were exported.

STRUGGLE FOR INDEPENDENCE

Because of the battles with the French for extended periods, the colonies and England grew close. There prevailed a healthy and friendly relationship. For over 150 years the colonies developed their own society, value systems, economy, and attempts at self-governance. England did not interfere in the settlement's affairs. They first provided security by keeping the British Armies in the settlements. But after the 1763-Paris treaty, there was a perceptible change in the British policy towards the colony. Direct taxes were levied. More and more coercive restrictions on manufacturing and trade were slapped on. Colonial assemblies and local governments enjoyed, hitherto, the right to tax. They did not like England interfering with their rights. They appealed for their rights; not for independence.

The answer from King George III of Great Britain was a cascade of more stringent restrictions. More troops were sent to maintain law and order and enforce the new measures strictly. These measures forced the colonies to think in terms of total independence from England. In 1765, a Quartering Act demanded colonies to provide housing and supplies to British troops. This was followed by another act – the Stamp Act. On the basis of this Act a direct tax on business instruments, licenses, legal documents and on newspapers was levied.

Due to extreme resentment shown by the colonies, this Stamp Act was repealed in the year 1766. However, new taxes – Townsend Duties – on glass, lead paint, paper and imported tea were levied. Colonies resented these sort of British coercive measures. They wanted to preserve their rights, liberty, duty and dignity, which over the years had become the hallmark of American people. In 1770, the Townsend duties were revoked. Only tax on tea remained. 1771, 1772 and 1773 were years that saw increasing tension between the colonies and Britain.

In 1773, the Tea Act was passed by England in their Parliament. This lead to the first ever-open resistance to English Rule; 342 tea chests were thrown into the sea from the anchored British ships in Boston. This resulted in the British passing the "Five Intolerable Acts," in the year 1774.

The first continental congress of the colonies met at Philadelphia and declared the Five Intolerable Acts as unconstitutional. The first battle took place in Massachusetts in the year 1775. The American Revolution, the war to end an oppressive regime, and with it, to end colonialism, had started. The second continental congress met again in Philadelphia and made George Washington the commander-in-chief of the continental forces. British troops defeated the continental forces.

On July 4, 1776, the Congress adopted one of the most famous documents in the United States History, prepared by Thomas Jefferson – **"The Declaration of Independence."** The turning point of revolution came when joint British and German forces under John Burgoyne were made to surrender at Saratoga. Still the United States forces and British troops continued to fight. In 1781, Lord Cornwallis lead a large contingent of British troops, which was resisted by George Washington, who was assisted by the French troops under commander Lafayette on the land and Admiral DeGrasse on sea. Cornwallis surrendered on October 19, 1781. The Peace Treaty signed at Paris by both France and England in 1783 formally granted independence to the United States.

There were 13 independent state governments with a central agency in the form of the Continental Congress. In 1781 this was replaced by the first National Government under the Articles of Confederation duly ratified by the 13 states. However, states were independent and strong and people's loyalty was always with their state, rather than the Federation. To correct this anomaly, delegates from all the states except Rhode Island met at Philadelphia in the year 1787. There they drafted the United States Constitution and the country has since been governed by it. By the middle of 1788, nine states had approved the constitution. A new law of the land had come into force.

BEGINNING OF UNITED STATES DEMOCRACY

In 1789 George Washington was elected as the first President of the United States. During his tenure the first ten amendments to the Constitution – the Bill of Rights – were made. In 1791, George Washington himself selected the site for the new capital of the country, which was fittingly named after him. The other Presidents who served during that time period were:

President	Important Events
1797-1800: John Adams	Washington refused a third time which had become an unbroken tradition till 1940. Adams, a Federalist, lacked charisma and his "Alien and sedition Acts" drew antagonism.

1801-1808: Thomas Jefferson	A Democrat, he is considered one of the chief architects of American Democracy. He added more territory. "The principle of Judicial Review of legislation" became a guiding principle which was an outcome of the Supreme Court's declaration of an act of Congress Unconstitutional. In 1807 The Congress halted import of slaves into U.S.
1809-1817: James Madison	War of 1812 against Britain, the war of 1815 at New Orleans and the Treaty of Ghent.
1818-1823: James Monroe	Known as "era of good feeling." More territories added. To stop the European and South American interference, the "Monroe Doctrine" was proclaimed in 1823.
1824: John Quincy Adams	House of representatives named Adams as President as none of the contesting candidates got a majority of electoral votes.
1828-1835: Andrew Jackson	He was identified with the common people, strengthened the Federal Government.
1836-1839: Martin Van Buren	His tenure saw a relentless depression. Whig Party was born.
1840: William Henry Harrison	Whig Party President. Short-lived Presidency. He died after 1 month of assuming office.
1840: John Tyler	William Henry Harrison's Vice-President. A milestone is the Oregon Trail. Railroads, Telegraphs, canals established. Democrat. Texas annexed.
1845: James Polk	"Mexican War" started. The treaty of Guadalupe-Hidalgo ended that war in 1848. New Mexico and California were ceded by Mexico as a result.
1849: Zachary Taylor	Whig President. Hero of Mexican War. Died very early in office.

| 1849: Millard Fillmore | Caught in the web of slavery issue. Congress passed "Compromise of 1850." California was made a free state. New Mexico and Utah slave states; that fact was not mentioned. |

ALASKA PURCHASE

As the United States was expanding westward across the American Continent, starting in 1725, Russia was seeking a foothold on the American continent as well. However, their interest started primarily on the Pacific side of the country with what is now Alaska. With its rich natural resources and sparse population, Russia hoped to establish their own place in the New World. However, low funding by the Russian government prevented any large scale colonization and when wars increased their need for funds, Russia offered to sell the land to the United States.

They hoped that doing so would at least offset the expansion of their British rivals. With the Civil War about to start, the sale was delayed, but eventually Secretary of State William Seward accepted the deal. Over 650 thousand square miles of land was purchased for only 7.2 million dollars – approximately 9 cents a square mile. At the time the purchase was called "Seward's Folly," but when gold mines were discovered Alaska proved itself to be a valuable resource for the growing United States.

SLAVERY, FIGHT FOR EQUALITY, CIVIL WAR AND REUNIFICATION – 1850-1877

By 1850, the United States grew to house 23 million people. The vast expanse of the United States had varied climatic conditions, natural resources, social fabric and industries, business, local affairs, etc., were with the States while matters of common interest were held by the federal Government. Sustained growth brought in its wake differences between States.

The issue that was threatening the very fabric of the existence of U.S. democracy itself was slavery. Slaves were used extensively in the cotton and tobacco plantations of the South. The North became critical of slave bonding. They talked about abolishing slavery to maintain human dignity. Those people were known as Abolitionists. The 'compromise of 1850' allayed the Southern fears temporarily.

During the next ten years tension increased between the North and South on slavery, States rights, etc. In 1852, Franklin Pierce, a Democrat became the 14th President. His "Kansas-Nebraska" Act of 1854 aroused passions and resulted in the formation of Anti Slavery Republican Party. The North, South divide reached a feverish pitch during the

15th President – James Buchanan, a Democrat's tenure largely because of Supreme Courts' Dred Scott Decision. The North was furious.

In 1857 the raid on Harpers Ferry by John Brown alienated the South. Minnesota in 1858, Oregon in 1859 and Kansas in 1861 (all those three States opposed Slavery) were admitted to the United States. In 1860, Abraham Lincoln, a Republican candidate; was elected President. Angered South took direct action. South Carolina, Mississippi, Florida, Alabama, Georgia, Louisiana and Texas seceded form the United States. They got a new Government of their own known as "Confederate States of United States."

THE AMERICAN CIVIL WAR

Confederate forces fired on the Union-held Fort Sumter on April 12, 1861. This act was seen as a rebellion by Lincoln. He roped in 75,000 volunteers for Military Service. Four Southern States, – North Carolina, Arkansas, Virginia and Tennessee – enraged by this action, seceded from the Union.

There erupted a major battle in July 1861 between Confederate forces and the Union army at Bull Run (Manassas). The war went into many fronts, one by one, during 1862, 63, 64 and 65. Gen. Ulysses S. Grant fought and won many battles and finally the war for the Union. With the surrender of Gen. Joseph Johnston's confederate troops in Durham, N.C. on April 26, 1865 the Union Government scored a decisive win over the war. During the war, West Virginia and Nevada were added to the Union.

In 1864, Lincoln was re-elected but he was assassinated within a month. Andrew Johnson, Lincoln's Vice-President, became President. During his tenure, the 13th and 14th Amendments abolished Slavery and granted Civil Rights for all. Nebraska joined the Union in 1867 and Alaska was bought from Russia. In 1868, Ulysses S. Grant, the Civil War hero, became the new Republican President. Blacks were given right to vote by the 15th Amendment to the Constitution. The 38th State, Colorado, joined the Union. With Grant's exit in 1877, the Depression was also over.

United States History: Part II

INDUSTRIAL AND INFRASTRUCTURAL GROWTH

In 1877, Rutherford B. Hayes became President. A vast industrial and business expansion took place. The next 30 years saw the country establishing 400,000 kilometers of railroad. Telephone & telegraph systems were established and a new faster method of printing took shape. North Dakota, South Dakota, Washington and Montana joined the

Union. Cities were growing rapidly. Immigrants in the millions came to United States to share the prosperity. James Garfield became the President in 1881.

The same year Garfield was felled by an assassin's bullet. Chester A. Arthur became president. In 1884, Grover Cleveland, a Democrat, came to the presidency, ending 24 years of Republican Rule. In 1888, he lost to Benjamin Harrison. However, Arthur again became president in 1892. In 1896, William McKinley, Republican, became President. He was re-elected in 1900 on a "full dinner pail" slogan. In 1904, Theodore Roosevelt was elected President. In 1908 William H. Taft won the presidency. Spanish-American war of 1898 saw U.S. gain Spanish colonies in Philippines and Puerto Rico. Then U.S. annexed Hawaii. In 1912, Woodrow Wilson, a Democrat, became president. He created new banking and currency systems controlled by Federal Reserve Board. The Federal Trade Commission was established. The 16th Amendment was passed which made it possible for federal income tax. The 17th Amendment made senators able to win election by a direct popular vote. Wilson also lowered duties through legislation. In 1913, World War I broke out in Europe.

WORLD WAR I – THE MOST POWERFUL NATION

Archduke Francis Ferdinand of Austria was assassinated on the June 28, 1914 resulting in the starting of war. Austria, Bulgaria, Germany, Hungry and Turkey – The Central Powers – were pitted against 23 Allied nations who were lead by France and Britain.

As the wide-spread military activity of WWI commenced in Europe, the United States sought to maintain strict neutrality in the matter. However, in April of 1917 it was no longer possible to remain neutral, and Congress made an official declaration of war against Germany. The two primary events that led to US entrance into the war were the unrestricted submarine warfare of Germany and the Zimmerman Telegram.

The submarine was a new development of WWI and the Germans used their new weapon to its greatest advantage in sinking the ships of its British and French opponents. However, when American merchant ships were caught in the cross-fires as well, it created a lot of tension between the U.S. and Germany. For a time, the submarine warfare slowed as the Germans sought to appease U.S. politicians. When military advisors insisted that the war could be ended within five months if submarines were used to their full potential, the submarine warfare resumed without restrictions. Even ships flying the U.S. flag were made targets in efforts to cripple trade, and as the deaths at sea increased President Woodrow Wilson began taking measures to prepare for war.

The final straw, however, was the Zimmerman Telegram. This was a telegram sent from Germany to Mexico. It was encouraging the Mexican government to attack the Southern border of the United States. The telegram was intercepted by the British and transmitted to the United States. With such an outright act of war, President Wilson went to Congress and asked for a declaration of war. On April 6, 1917 the United States officially entered the conflict.

The United States dispatched over two million men to Europe and sent its formidable Navy to the European sea to fight along with the Allies. General John J. Pershing led the AEF (United American Expeditionary Force) and after a few battles fought the greatest battle at Meuse-Argonne.

On November 11, 1918, Germany asked for an armistice. Wilson put forth the idea of "a League of Nations" which was voted out by the Senate. War had made the U.S. an arsenal of most sophisticated weaponry. Its air power as well as sea power was awesome. World War I had seen the birth of a superpower.

WORLDWIDE DEPRESSION AND WORLD WAR II

Warren G. Handing became the President on a Republican platform. He died in 1923 and Calvin Coolidge better known as "Silent Cal" became President and won the 1924 election as well.

The time of the election, the 1920s, is considered as a prosperous decade. Skyscrapers were built. There was a general boom all-round. Schools, colleges and universities expanded.

The matter of gender equality in the United States has been a popular topic of feminists throughout the 1900s. An Equal Rights Amendment which would constitutionally mandate that there could be no discrimination on a basis of gender was first proposed in 1923. By the 1960s, a strong push by feminist groups to get the amendment passed brought a new wave of support.

As a result the amendment –which passed in both the House and the Senate – was sent to the states for approval. It wasn't long before 30 of the necessary 38 states had voted in favor of the agreement. However, a strong opposition developed led primarily by a woman named Phyllis Schlafly. She took action and wrote an article called What's Wrong with the Equal Rights Amendment, which quickly gained the approval of conservatives across the nation. She organized rallies, baked bread for legislators, hung "Don't Draft Me" signs on baby girls, and appeared on television all in an effort to prevent the passage of the amendment. She argued that the amendment would destroy conservative family values, eliminate alimony and other protective laws, and strongly disadvantage full time homemakers. Due in large part to her efforts, the amendment was never passed.

President Hoover took office in 1929. By October, the Stock Market crashed. The United States was pulled into the World Wide Depression steadily. Industries came to a grinding halt in the wake of total financial breakdown. Unemployment soared. Hoover failed had failed in trying to revive the economy.

Despite the fact that settlers came to the American continent in search of freedom, rarely was that same freedom was not extended to the Native American people already inhabiting the lands. As the country formed and continued to grow, the Native American populations were pushed further and further west, and agreements guaranteeing their safety and lands were violated again and again. For the Cherokee people, this eventually led to a mass migration over thousands of miles known as the Trail of Tears.

In the 1930s, Andrew Jackson signed into law the Removal Act. Tribes were forced to sign agreements which would allow the military and citizens of the southern states to "help" them relocate west of the Mississippi river. When the time for relocation came the people were forced from their homes at bayonet point, and many were beaten or raped. The people were forced to march 1,200 miles with thousands dying of disease and starvation along the way. Similar events were true for other tribes who were promised protection and preservation of their lands if they agreed to move to reservations. Many peacefully agreed to the arrangement, only to have their agreements broken and their lands taken from them.

In 1933, Franklin Delano Roosevelt, a Democrat, became President. His moves tied down further sliding of economy. He won re-election decisively. He scrapped prohibition. He was also responsible for The New Deal. **The New Deal reforms were at the root of all welfare legislation in the United States.** The most prominent among New Deal legislation was the Social Security Act of 1935 which aimed at unemployment compensation, aid to dependent children, old age assistance, aid to States for Pensions as well as grants to States for maternal services.

When Lyndon Johnson was the President, very laudable welfare legislations under the heading **"Great Society"** were attempted in 1960's.

Meanwhile, Benito Mussolini, a fascist, came to power in Italy. Adolf Hitler, a Nazi, came to power in Germany. His main agenda was to persecute Jews. In the Far East, Japan came under the control of Military Chiefs who ardently wanted to expand into Manchuria and China. Now Italy, Germany, and Japan became close and formed an Alliance known as the "Axis."

The United States did not want to participate in the war, but they did prepare very well to meet any eventuality. By 1939, the whole of Europe was struggling to evade Hitler's malicious attacks. The United States had to rescue Great Britain and France. Roosevelt sent 50 destroyers to England and got rights to build Naval and Air bases in the stretch from British Guiana to Newfoundland. Presidential elections came. Roosevelt was reelected. In the history of the United States, he became the only President to serve the nation for more than two terms.

Production of planes, ships, guns and other war-related products started at a frenetic pace. On December 7, 1941, the Japanese attacked the U.S. Naval base housed in Pearl Harbor and Hawaii. Germany and Italy declared war on the U.S. as per its agreement between member countries of the "Axis."

During WWII, riots broke out between Latino youths and military servicemen in the Los Angeles area. These were referred to as the Zoot Suit Riots because of the colorful apparel of the Latino youths. They mainly attacked Mexican-American Marines or Mexican-American Sailors, but other minorities were affected as well.

The U.S. had no option but to side with the "Allies." A large contingent of the Army was sent along with a huge number of fighter planes and warships. Gen. Dwight D. Eisenhower took command in Europe and advanced steadily against the Axis powers. On August 6, 1945, the first Nuclear Bomb was dropped on the city of Hiroshima, evaporating the city and its people in seconds. The Japanese emperor halted the war and asked the U.S. for peace. The U.S. had become a most admired as well as a terribly feared superpower.

During the final stages of the war, Roosevelt won his fourth term as President in the 1944 election. However, on April 12, 1945, after serving less than 100 days he died and his Vice-President, Harry S. Truman became the 33rd President. He worked hard to promote the United Nations organization.

THE COLD WAR ERA AND THEREAFTER

In 1947, an important law was enacted, which paved the way for the Nations Armed forces getting unified and work under a single Secretary of Defense. The Soviet Union started spreading after the war and the United States was alarmed at the speed with which communism was spreading. U.S. started giving aid to countries threatened by communism, which was not liked by the U.S.S.R. There were many conflicts between the U.S.S.R. and the western Allies.

In May 1949, the North Atlantic Treaty was ratified, which assured the member Nations common defense against any external aggression. On June 25, 1950, North Korea, a communist state, invaded South Korea. United States sent its army and navy to the South. China opposed this and the U.N. named China an aggressor. In 1951, the Soviet Union proposed a ceasefire. After the war, most of West Germany was held by France, the United Kingdom, the United States and the U.S.S.R. The territories of France, the United Kingdom and the United States merged to form F.R.G. – Federal Republic of Germany. The U.S.S.R. which held East Germany became G.D.R. – German Democratic Republic. By a peace agreement in 1951, Allied occupation came to an end in West Germany. General Dwight Eisenhower, the war hero, became the Republican President in 1952. The first nuclear-powered submarine was commissioned in the year 1954, named "Nautilus." In 1953 he signed a truce in Korea after a little over two years of peace talks. In 1954, Eisenhower got reelected as President. The United States, the U.S.S.R. and the U.K. discussed disarmament and banning of Nuclear Tests with no results.

On October 4, 1957, Soviet Union sent a satellite – Sputnik 1 – and the U.S. thought it wise to spend more on space research. In January 1958, the Explorer 1 satellite was sent out by the United States. In Cuba, Fidel Castro overthrew the then dictator by a revolution and set up a communist regime and became friendly with the Russians. In 1960, John F. Kennedy won the Presidential election. The Soviet Union with the help of friendly Castro, kept nuclear missiles in Cuba aimed at the United States and South America. In 1961, the Bay of Pigs invasion took place. This was an effort to place military trained Cuban exiles back on the island to over throw Castro's regime. The attempt was unsuccessful. Kennedy worked hard for human dignity and equality. He was assassinated on November 22, 1963, in Dallas.

When President John F Kennedy was assassinated in 1963, his Vice President Lyndon B Johnson became President of the United States. Johnson moved quickly to enact two important elements of Kennedy's presidency: the Civil Rights Act of 1964 and the Economic Opportunity Act of 1964. These two widely supported acts helped him to gain a political foothold. There were only 11 months until the next election, giving Johnson little time to build a campaign.

The center of his campaign and his presidency was the idea of a "Great Society." Johnson's challenge to the American people was to build a "great society" and seek to cure many of the traditional ills of poverty and misfortune. He won the election with the greatest popular margin in history - 15 million votes.

Over the next four years he went on to pass over 200 bills as part of the "Great Society" campaign. These included the Wilderness Protection Act which saved millions of acres of forests, Elementary and Secondary Education Acts, Voting Rights Acts, Medicare, Immigration Acts, and many other acts aimed at alleviating troubling social conditions.

During his presidency, Johnson improved health care and education, worked to alleviate poverty and homelessness, and championed civil rights. The greatest troubling aspect of his presidency was the war in Vietnam. He chose not to run for a second term in office – stating that he wanted to continue working for peace without the troubles of the office. However, he died of a sudden heart attack before the war came to a conclusion.

In 1968, Martin Luther King Jr. was killed and more riots followed. The anti-communist stand of the United States during the 1960's increasingly drew the country towards the Vietnam War. South Vietnam was supported by the United States while the communist, rebel Viet Cong were supported by North Vietnam. By 1968 there were more than half-a-million United States troops fighting in Vietnam. In 1968, Richard M. Nixon, a Republican, became the President. He proposed withdrawal of troops from Vietnam in a phased manner. In 1972, Nixon was reelected. By early 1973 United States withdrew all its troops. That war cost more than 200 billion dollars and 50,000 lives.

On July 1969, Apollo-II mission's astronauts landed on the moon. Soon, the Watergate scandal broke out. Nixon was accused of sending agents to break into Democratic National Committee Headquarters at Watergate Complex to spy on their activities. Public sentiment was against Nixon's continuance. He resigned on August 8, 1974 and his deputy Gerald Ford became President. Inflation, unemployment, recession, stagnation continued from Nixon's tenure into Ford's Presidency.

Next, Jimmy Carter won the elections and became President. In 1977 Anwar el-Sadat of Egypt visited Jerusalem, Israel. He was the first Arab head to do so. Carter brought China closer to the U.S. and entered into full diplomatic relations in 1979. He signed the SALT-II (Strategic Arms Limitation Talks II) with Leonid I Brezhnev. An anti-American fundamentalist, Ayatollah Ruhollah Khomeini, came to power after the Shah's Regime in Iran was overthrown by a revolution.

The United States Embassy in Tehran was taken over by a mob and everyone inside was taken hostage. Carter froze all Iranian assets in the U.S. and said he would release the funds only after the hostages were released.

In the end of the year 1979, Soviet troops invaded Afghanistan. Carter cut off grain exports and high tech equipment sales to the U.S.S.R. By early 1980, the United States had come under the grip of a mild recession. Ronald Reagan became President in 1980. He got the U.S. embassy hostages in Iran released. Unemployment figures almost reached double figures. He authored S.D.I. (Strategic Defense Initiative) to safeguard men and material of the U.S. from foreign attack. Soviets started an arsenal build-up on the Grenada Island. Reagan invaded Grenada and took control.

He became a hero in the United States, but a fiend in foreign countries. In the 1984 election, Reagan prevailed. After a long history of mutual hatred and belligerent attitudes, the United States and the U.S.S.R. met at a summit meeting in 1985 at Geneva. There was no meaningful accord. Reagan and Gorbachev met for a third time in Washington D.C. during December 1987. There was an accord on the reduction of intermediate-range nuclear forces (INF) in Europe.

In January of 1986, Reagan imposed economic sanction against Libya for having perpetrated terrorist attacks on the United States. Reagan's regime had the dubious distinction of increasing the national debt from 914 billion to over 2.5 trillion.

George Bush became the next Republican President. He showed more interest in foreign affairs. He sent troops to Panama to depose the then Dictator Gen. Manuel Noriega. Communist regions in Eastern Europe collapsed. In 1990, West and East Germany were reunited. He continued to have good relations with Soviet Union. In December 1991, the U.S.S.R. fell apart into disunited small states. It was the end of the so-called cold war. In August 1990, Iraq under Saddam Hussein, invaded Kuwait.

The Persian Gulf War continued for five weeks and ended in early 1991. The Arabs and Israelis were persuaded to come to the negotiating table. By the middle of 1990, the recession began to show its ugly face yet again. In 1992, Bill Clinton, a Democrat, won the Presidency. The North America Free Trade Agreement (NAFTA) between the United States, Canada and Mexico was signed. A deficit reduction passage and a family leave act were passed. He sent forces to Bosnia and Herzegovina and persuaded them for talks to end that country's civil war. In 1996, Clinton was reelected. The economy during his tenure was strong and continued to grow during his second term also.

In 1996, the United States registered the largest Budget Surpluses in the history of the nation. His only blemish was on moral turpitude, which saw him impeached but he was not removed from office.

NATO, lead by the United States and England, bombed Kosovo to end the Serbian aggression against native Albanians. It was a success. Clinton tried his best to find a peaceful settlement between Palestinians and Israel.

George W. Bush, son of the former President George Bush, became President. He brought in a 1.35 trillion dollar Tax-cut Bill, which became law in June 2001. On September 11, 2001, terrorists hijacked four commercial planes and crashed two on the Twin Towers of the World Trade Center in New York, one into the Pentagon in Washington D.C. and the last one into the fields in Pennsylvania. Al Qaeda and its leader Osama Bin Laden were blamed. Bush invaded Afghanistan as there was enough proof to show that the Taliban Government there encouraged Al Qaeda and its leaders. By end of 2001, the Taliban Government lost its power and its leaders started running for their lives. Domestic security had never been given so much importance as then. Bush also accused Iraqi leader Saddam Hussein of having nuclear and chemical and biological warfare material. He felt Iraq was producing nuclear weapons. The United States attacked Iraq and finally got hold of Hussein as a Prisoner of war. He was later executed following a guilty verdict at his trial. Bush was re-elected for another term as President.

UNITED STATES HISTORY – POINTS TO REMEMBER

- 1539 – First land journey into the continent – Hernando De Soto – a Spaniard landed in Florida.
- 1619 – Virginia got its House of Burgesses (citizens). This was the first represen- tative assembly known to have existed in the U.S.
- 1619 – First batch of Blacks arrived in United States Colonies.
- 1620 – The second English colony was established in Plymouth.
- 1620 – Capt. Miles Standish landed with 100 people in a place which is today known as Massachusetts. His ship was the Mayflower.
- 1649 – Maryland passed Religious Toleration Act – first of its kind in the colonies.
- 1763 – The Treaty of Paris formally put a stop to frequent French/Indian and English settlers' war.
- 1764 – The first law to collect money from American Colonies by the British was enacted in British Parliament.
- 1770 – Five Americans were killed by the British soldiers in Boston and this in- cident was called "The Boston Massacre of 1770."
- 1774 – The Boston Tea Party – 342 chests of tea was thrown into the sea by the Colonists. This was the first open resistance against the British.
- 1776 – Thomas Paine of Philadelphia was the first to openly call for independence.
- 1787 – Ordinance of 1787 or Northwest Ordinance ranks next only to Declaration of Independence and the Constitution.
- 1789 – The eleven colonies elected the first ever President of the U.S. – George Washington became the first President with John Adams as his Vice-President.
- 1791 – During Washington's period, the first 10 amendments to the Constitution – the Bill of Rights were enacted.
- 1796 – Washington refused a 3rd term which had become an unwritten code for future Presidents to follow, unbroken, until 1940.
- 1846 – The 49th Parallel to the Pacific was agreed to be the boundary line between the United States and Canada.
- 1854 – The Kansas Nebraska Act of 1854 brought in by Franklin Pierce resulted in the organization of the anti-slavery Republican Party.
- 1861 – the first ever telegraph connection was established across the continent.
- 1863 – Abraham Lincoln's "Emancipation Proclamation" freed no less than 3 million slaves in the U.S.
- 1868 – President Andrew Johnson escaped conviction of impeachment charges by a mere single vote in the senate.
- 1869 – During Ulysses S. Grant's Presidency, the first ever network of railroads was completed. Golden Spike was driven in Utah on May 10, 1869.
- 1914 – The Panama Canal was opened.

- 1919 – the 18th Amendment to the constitution established Prohibition through out the U.S.
- 1924 – San Francisco to New York City airmail service started.
- 1927 – Charles A. Lindbergh flew alone across the Atlantic.
- 1940 – Franklin Delano Roosevelt was reelected in 1940, for a third term, breaking the hitherto followed tradition of an incumbent President not seeking a third term.
- 1945 – President Harry S. Truman presided over the victory in the Second World War in Europe. Truman signed the order of nuclear bombing over Hiroshima and Nagasaki.
- 2001 – On September 11, 2001, four planes were hijacked by Terrorists and two of those crashed on the towering Twin Towers of the World Trade Center in New York.

Western Civilization

DIVINE RIGHT

Throughout the medieval and early modern period, one of the most powerful ways that monarchies asserted their authority was through the doctrine of the divine right of kings. This is a belief that the right of the king to rule is given directly by God. As a result, they both speak for God and answer to no one but Him.

The habit of many rulers to speak in terms of "we" derives from this logic. When the king would decree something it wasn't just him, it was both him and God. This proved a powerful form of propaganda because it inherently implies that if a person commits treason than they are truly acting out against God and placing their souls in jeopardy. For centuries kings used this argument to solidify their positions of power.

ANCIENT WESTERN ASIA, GREECE AND ROME

The most recent ice age began some 1.6 million years ago and ended 10,000 years ago. In the history of Earth, there were certain periods when the climates became so cold as to form extensive ice sheets. These periods are called ice-ages. Prehistoric humans lived on the continent of Europe as long ago as the recent ice age. Asian and Egyptian civilizations converged into Europe some 4,000 years ago. Greek and Roman Empires are the starting point of European recorded history. Over centuries of phased progress, the Roman Empire had to be bifurcated into two fragments, immediately after the demise of their Great Emperor, Theodosius, way back in 395 AD.

Before the formation of the Republic, Roman Society was divided into two classes:

- Patricians
- Plebeians

Patricians were the upper class landlords, aristocrats, and wealthy businessmen. Plebeians were small landlords, farmers and small businessmen. Plebeians were of foreign origin and settled in different cities of Rome. Senate and magistrate offices were under the direct hold of Patricians. Plebeians were exploited by the patricians to work on their lands, pay heavy taxes and to fight for them in wars. Plebeians had no rights in senate but were members of the assembly.

Plebeians' uprising gained momentum in 494 BC and they forced Patricians to elect Tribunes, a local plebeian officer who could veto the decision of Magistrate.

In 450 BC, 12 tables of law were published because of plebeian protest, which gave citizens of Rome the right to appeal.

In 367 BC, the first plebeian council was elected. Plebeians were also eligible to contest for Magistrate.

PUNIC WARS

Rome fought three wars with Carthage, famous as Punic Wars of Rome. Carthage was a Great Empire on the northern coast of Africa. Their enormous wealth and strong navy envied the Romans. Moreover, Carthage was an ambitious empire and whose expansion created trouble for Rome.

The Roman Empire was well known for his disciplined and terrifying legions. However, military power is not the only reason that the empire was so successful in expansion. They also took advantage of resources and cultures in the nations they claimed. The model of Roman expansion-particularly early on- involved establishing conquered lands as "client states."

The idea of this model is that conquered nations become subjugated to the parent nation. To a large extent, the peoples conquered by Rome were allowed to continue on their business as usual (with an increase in taxes to support the Roman legions and rulers). Politically, however, the people became subject to Roman-placed rulers and laws. In return for allowing this subjugation, Rome offered protection from outside invasions.

This model allowed Rome to expand rapidly and it became one of the great nations in history. After reaching a certain point, however, expansion proved incredibly difficult.

Rome relied on the resources of client nations to support increases in military and government. However, as it moved farther into Northern Europe there was little to be found in terms of silver, gold, and precious metals.

The empire simply couldn't afford to keep expending military effort in those areas. To the east lay the formidable Parthian empire. The Parthian empire was a similarly powerful and formidable opponent and became an effective barrier to Roman expansion in the East. Although as emperor Trajan was able to conquer a small amount of Parthian territory, for the most part Rome was never successful in wholly defeating the Parthians.

First War with Carthage broke out in 264 BC. It was also known as the first Punic War. It lasted for 23 years and Rome emerged as the victorious state.

Second Punic War was fought in 218 BC when Carthaginians tried to build a Spanish Empire. This war lasted for 16 years and ended with Carthage surrendering most of its territory, assets and paying three times more indemnification as paid in first War of Carthage. Hannibal, the great Carthaginian General led this war on behalf of Carthage.

Third Punic War was fought between 149-146 BC. It was the bloodiest Punic War and ended with the devastation of Carthage and all its citizens being enslaved.

JULIUS CAESAR (100-44 BC)

Caesar's fame started to grow with his victories over Gaul. At one time, Caesar was announced as the enemy of state by the conspiracies of Pompey, his political rival whom he defeated in 48 BC in Pharsalus.

Caesar conquered Asia Minor soon after defeating Pompey. In 46 BC, he declared himself as the next ruler of Rome. He was assassinated by a group of conspirers in 44 BC.

ROME IN THIRD CENTURY

Imperial rule of the great Roman Empire came to an end in the third century. Marcus Aurelius was the last successful king among the Five Good Emperors. He was succeeded by Commodus.

TRADE IN THIRD CENTURY

Roman trade expanded to nearly all parts of the world including India, Arabia and China. Items like clothes, artifacts and glass were exported at that time. Heavy export of these goods did not make any contribution to the prosperity of Rome. Roman Economy crippled and wealth distributed highly unevenly.

Availability of slaves declined and hence production too. On the other hand, imports for the luxury of rich and elite were too heavy to be countered by domestic export. Consequently, Roman Economy began to crush under own imports.

GERMAN INVASION

In third century, Roman Civilization faced two assaults, one from Christianity and another from Germans. German invaders were always a threat for Roman Civilization. Diocletian and Theodosius the great were successful in keeping Germans away from Rome, but their successors failed to do so. By fifth century, Germans invaded all western Rome.

German invaders, also called as barbarians by some historians, were similar to Romans in many ways. Although they were illiterate and did not live in cities like Romans, their appearance and customs were much similar to that of neighboring Romans. Living for centuries in close vicinity of Rome, has left some impression on them. Primarily, they were hunters and grazers but they did practice some sort of cultivation to meet their food needs. Unlike Romans who used copper, Germans used iron for making jewelry and pottery.

Geographical conditions were also responsible for German invasion. Rome and Germany were situated next to each other with only Rhine and Danube separating them. Rome has long trading history with some of the German tribes. More than often, leftover Roman fields were acquired by the bordering tribes of Germany.

Germans played an important role in Roman warfares by allying with Roman armies to fight other Germanic tribes.

The most important thing that brought Germans more close to Rome was the adoption of Christianity. By the onset of Fourth Century, most of the German tribes adopted the heretical Arian Christianity. They no longer considered themselves as barbarians. Hence their ambition for getting into the heart of Rome gained even more momentum.

Ruling Rome was not the primary motive of Germans. They were looking for more lands that can give them better yields every year. In the last quarter of Fourth Century, tribe of Visigoths revolted against Roman officials and finally defeated their army in the war of Adrianople.

After the victory of Adrianople in 378 AD, Germans formed friendly relations with the ruling emperor of Rome, Theodosius the great and remained on friendly terms till his death. After the death of Theodosius in 395 AD, his kingdom was divided among his two incompetent sons.

Alaric, the leader of Visigoths at that time acted wisely and selected best lands and provisions for his tribe. Very soon, a great portion of Rome was acquired by Germans much to the envy of their neighbors.

In 406 AD, Vandals and Visigoths lead a combined attack on Gaul to enter straight into Spain. After sometime, they crossed the straits into the north western territories of Roman Africa. At that time, it was the most heavily harvested land of the Roman Empire and the victory brought Rome to its knees. German march of victory did not end there. They also won Central Mediterranean by defeating Roman Navy in 455 AD.

Last blow to the great civilization of Rome came in the year 476, when a group of Germans sacked the non-existent king of Rome, Augustulus, a boy in his teens, to gain control of the entire Rome, forever.

MEDIEVAL HISTORY

In 700, three civilizations emerged from different parts of Mediterranean Sea – Byzantine, Islam and western Christian. All these were considered as successors of Roman civilization. The story of Byzantine civilization had many twists and turns. The origin of the Byzantine Empire is not clear yet, but is believed that this civilization succeeded the Roman civilization.

The arrival of the Justinian's reign had great impact upon the Byzantine civilization as it marked the beginning of new thoughts and practices.

Factors responsible for the stability of the Byzantine Empire

The most important cause for the stability of the Byzantine Empire was the intricate and tricky backstage machination. Another reason was the highly efficient and active bureaucrats. The third factor was the stable economic firms. Despite the decline of urban life in most of the western countries, the eastern part of Byzantine had a solid commerce and city life. The Byzantine Empire had also good source of income through their silk-making business.

Agriculture during the Byzantine civilization was of great importance as it was the biggest source of income. The concept of free peasantry vanished with the arrival of aristocrats in 1025 AD.

Byzantine civilization is also remembered for its religious beliefs and practices. The Byzantine civilization had a complicated religious dimension, as the emperors of those days had interfered in the working of the church. It was during the eighth century, religious practices saw some stability because of the decline if many eastern provinces.

Another issue related to the religion of Byzantine civilization was the iconoclastic. The iconoclasts strongly believed that images made by man himself cannot be worshipped, and Christ is so great that no one can portray his exact image, thus worshipping icons should be prohibited.

Byzantine civilization had some very special things. One is that Byzantine civilization showed equal concern to Greek teachings and Christianity. It also contributed a lot for women's education.

Architecture During Byzantine Civilization

The architecture of this period can best be realized through Church of Santa Sophia. It symbolizes the inward and spiritual character of the Christian religion. The structure of this monument was different from others constructed at that time. Most of the art and architecture of the Byzantine civilization were based on the ancient Greek style. The Byzantines were popularly remembered for their ivory paintings, jewelry making and creation of mosaics. A mosaic is a picture, which is made by assembling several small pieces of glass or stone.

With the passage of time, Byzantines' ties with Russia improved. But, its relations with the West were bitter. In 1204, when Constantinople was sacked, its relation with the West became worse. Taking the advantage of the situation, Turks conquered Constantinople in 1453.

The hatred of Byzantine for Islam helped the West to preserve Greek learning.

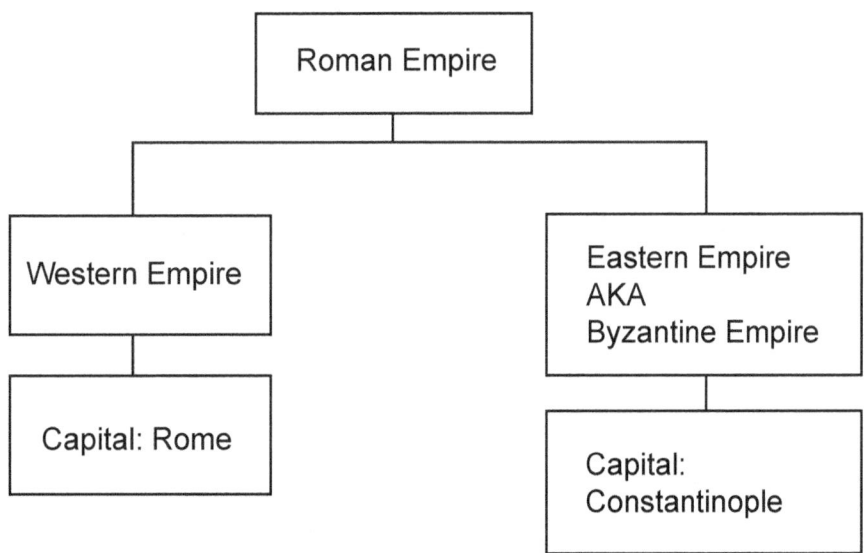

Visigoths and Ostrogoths (The Gothic Tribes) were living for over 200 years in the areas between the Danube and the Black Sea. The Huns of Central Asia invaded the region occupied by the Goths, who had no alternative but to go in the Western direction. (The great Gothic Invasion of 375 AD). Visigoths, Burgundians, and Franks, members of Germanic Tribes, got hold of the Gaul region (today's West Germany, Northern Italy, France and a few parts of Belgium). Visigoths, Suevi and Vandals (Germanic Tribes) moved to Spain, while good many vandals moved over to Northern Africa. Briton, once a Roman garrison, but abandoned in 410 AD became a hunting ground for Anglos and Saxons. However, the Roman Empire had left an indelible mark on Europe in the area of its culture, law, language as well as governance. Greece and Rome were part of Mediterranean Europe. The continent's political supremacy passed from Mesopotamia to Greece and from Greece to Rome. Then it passed on to Spain and Portugal and finally to Western Europe. Southern Europe by and large was neglected.

MEDIEVAL EUROPE

The Treaty of Verdun, 843 AD, agreed to divide the Frankish empire between the grandsons of Charlemagne was the beginning of the nations of Germany and France. The German empire was reinvigorated by the King, Otto I, and became the Holy Roman Empire by 962 AD. In 1453, Ottoman Turks invaded Constantinople. The Gothic's uni- fied Castile, Aragon and Leon and named the Kingdom "The Catholic Sovereigns of Spain" in the early 15th century.

Vikings built settlements in 850 AD, in the Western regions of France. During 1066 AD, Normans, a new dynasty, descendants of Vikings, not only ruled England but added Sicily and Naples to their lands. France gradually became powerful and Louis XI, during the 15th century, made it the first strong Monarchy. Christianity spread.

In 1494, Charles VIII of France fought a series of wars over Sicily and Naples against Italy. France, Spain and Italy were fighting for over 50 years. Charles V, the Emperor of Holy Roman Empire, at the end of that protracted war had added in addition to Spain, Germany and Sardinia got Sicily, Naples, the Netherlands, Burgundy, Milan and a few regions of the New World.

Phillip II and his descendants lost their grip gradually, paving the way for Protestants. Reformation started by Martin Luther asserted their superiority over the weakened Catholics. The Thirty-year War (1618-48 AD) of Catholic and Protestant Rulers made the Holy Roman Empire powerless and drained. They had only Austria and Germany to contend with. In the meantime, France asserted itself and became the first major power in Europe. Sweden invaded Germany, Poland and Russia.

In the 18th century, Peter the Great and Catherine II of Russia, made it an awesome power. The French Revolution started in 1789. Poland was partitioned by its neighbors.

Prussia, under Frederick the Great had became a formidable power. England had become home to the British Empire.

During Industrial Revolution, many English inventions and innovations benefited mankind. The French revolution brought changes in its wake. Napoleon I fought many wars and annexed parts of Germany, parts of Italy, the Netherlands and parts of Dalmatia.

Waterloo in 1815 saw the ignominious defeat of Napoleon and France was made to revert to its earlier territory. An emaciated Germany with only 38 states, which included Prussia and Austria, became a union known as the "German Confederation."

The Czar of Russia, Alexander I in the year 1815, spelled out an ambiguous draft treaty, which he called a "Holy Alliance" in which he assured all Monarchs of Europe that only the conduct specified in the Christian religion be followed. However, Austria, Russia, Great Britain and Prussia formed during the same year a "Quadruple Alliance or, Grand Alliance" for the purpose of retaining a hereditary Government. France also was admitted into the Alliance later. No worthwhile change could be made with the approval of these great powers. The French Revolution changed that equation.

French Monarchs, in due course were hated by the people and the Revolution started, which spread to other countries. The Industrial Revolution followed, which brought in its wake prosperity to the common man. In 1848, a sort of republic was set up in France. France helped to free Italy from Sardinia.

Otto Von Bismark, the Prime Minister of Prussia, made Austria come out of the German Confederation. A Despot-Queen Isabella of Spain was sent packing by the people and Spain became a Republic. Italy also drove away her absolute monarchs and brought in their place democratic monarchs. The Industrial Revolution made many goods easy and cheap to produce.

MODERN EUROPE

Russia spread towards most of Northern Asia. Britain established colonies in a number of countries. On June 28, 1914, Austria's crown prince Francis Ferdinand was assassinated, which resulted in a war with Serbia. Russia sided with Serbia, being the protector of Slavic states. Then Germany, Austria-Hungary and Italy on the one side and Great Britain, France and Russia on the opposite side started what was known as World War I. The war brought in its wake extensive changes in Europe. Boundaries were altered. The Czar of Russia was killed by the mob desiring a Soviet system under Lenin. Austria and Germany dethroned their Emperors. In Turkey, Mustafa Kemal, drove the then Sultan out of power and established the Republic of Turkey. War-torn European Governments were economically ruined. Germany's awesome land, sea and air power were reduced by the Treaty of Versailles. The rebuilding of Europe started.

During the 1920's business showed tremendous improvement. Most war-torn countries continued to maintain their existing system of democratic Governance. Dictatorship reared its ugly head in some countries. Russia came under Communism, Germany under Adolf Hitler and Italy under Benito Mussolini. Poland, Spain and Austria and a number of Balkan States embraced a socialistic form of governance. Italy and Germany joined hands to support each other through the "Rome-Berlin" Axis. Later Japan also joined them through what is known as the "Anti-Comintern" accord. In early 1938, Hitler invaded Austria. Italy and Germany helped the rebels of the Spanish civil war and General Francisco Franco seized power on March 28, 1939. His was a Fascist dictatorship and he joined the "Anti-Comintern" pact. Hitler invaded Poland on September 1, 1939. England and France declared a war on Germany. Soviets were not taking sides initially.

But when Hitler started intrusion into Soviet Union, they joined the Allies -England, France on June 21, 1941. Japan had the audacity to attack Pearl Harbor on December 7, 1941, which thoughtless action brought the hitherto neutral United States to the side of Allies. The Allies were strengthened and defeated the Axis Powers.

In August 1945, Communism and socialism on the one side and Democracies on the other side vied for power in Europe. The Allies had established the United Nations to keep countries away from war and hold perpetual peace. NATO was formed in 1949 with most countries of Western Europe plus Canada and United States. From 1989 onwards, Governments of Eastern Europe started shunning Communism. The great U.S.S.R. disappeared into smaller independent states. Communism fell in Europe, but the world had to face a new variety of fear, terrorism! Terrorism, particularly the religious fanaticism-propelled variety, held sway in most countries and the high point was the decimation of the Twin Towers of World Trade Center in New York by crashing two hijacked passenger flights into it.

WESTERN CIVILIZATION – POINTS TO REMEMBER

- Charlemagne consolidated the Germanic invasion and built an Empire in 800 AD.
- In Spain, Islam was established, after 711 AD.
- Islam lost its pre-eminence after the Moors were defeated in 1492 AD.
- The Byzantine Empire was defeated by the Ottoman Turks in 1453 AD.
- The Bubonic plague (a.k.a. The Black Death) erased nearly 33% of European Population during the 14th century. This was easily spread by rats and fleas along the different trade routes.
- During the 19th century, the British Parliament was seen as the "Mother of Parliaments."
- Russia, Great Britain, Prussia, Austria and France dominated the "Concert" of Europe.

- The Crimean war (1854-56) started when Russia tried to invade Turkey.
- After the Franco-Prussian war of 1870-71 AD, Otto Von Bismarck annexed Alsace-Lorraine.
- The Balkan wars were the result of the Balkan States' war against Turkey.
- The Treaty of Versailles with Germany, saw the return of Alsace-Lorraine to France.
- In the year 1920, a Permanent Court of International Justice was set up in The Hague to settle international disputes.
- In 1925, the major powers of the world signed treaties (Locarno Treaties) agreeing not to expand their territories and ready to submit all disputes to the League System.
- 1933, Hitler announced withdrawal of Germany from the League.
- V.E. Day (Victory in Europe Day was celebrated by the Allies on May 8, 1945 when Germany surrendered).
- In August 1945, the Allied Powers had formed the United Nations (U.N.) largely to maintain peace in the world.
- The Organization of European Economic Co-operation (OEEC) was established in the year 1948.
- The Warsaw pact, a Treaty for mutual defense, was signed by East Germany, Po- land, Czechoslovakia, Bulgaria, Poland, Romania and Russia.
- Soviet Union signed an agreement with the United States and the U.K. to a Lim- ited Test Ban Treaty in 1963.
- Israeli athletes were attacked inside the Olympic Village in Munich (West Germany) by the "Black September" Terrorist organization of Palestine.
- Pan American Airlines flight 103 was bombed over Lockerbie in Scotland in the year 1988.
- The "Good Friday" Agreement of I.R.A. and the Government in 1998 saw IRA's abrogation of it weapons.
- "Glasnost" (openness) and "perestroika" (restructuring) policies of U.S.S.R.'s Mikhail Gorbachev brought in reforms in all governmental spheres.
- In the year 1989, East and West Germany were re-united.
- In late 1991, the Soviet Union suspended the predominance of the Communist Party and in December that year the Soviet Union ceased and became the Commonwealth of Independent States.
- In late 1992, Czechoslovakia dissolved its 75-year old federation and became the Czech Republic and Slovakia, two independent countries.
- The European Union (EU) is the unifying force in Europe and today they have their own currency known as the "Euro." The European Union is becoming stronger and stronger economically, though politically they are separate entities. The United Kingdom does NOT use the Euro.

World History

With all its catastrophic changes – natural calamities, unwanted wars, etc. – the twentieth century had done enough for mankind to cheer. Technological innovations, scientific inventions, economic strides – all these and more have enriched the lives of mankind as never before and the latest information explosion ushered in by information technology has made the standard of living go many notches up. We are in the middle of a unique Revolution, which is bringing in what is known as the "knowledge economy." Knowledge is becoming a power to contend with.

AFRICA

Africa is much larger than Europe as far as land goes. The discovery of the American continent by Columbus had sparked a strong wave of imperialism among European nations that continued into the later centuries. As industrial European markets grew there was a renewed desire to increase access to both natural resources and markets where the finished goods could be sold.

This led to the "Scramble for Africa" as European eyes turned toward the vast and still mostly unexplored continent of Africa. Rivalries between nations began to get heated and soon a conference was called by German Chancellor Otto von Bismarck for the purpose of partitioning the remaining unclaimed lands of Africa. This has become known as the Berlin Conference of 1884. The partitions were based on an agreement to spread Christianity, increase trade, and establish a physical presence in the regions (although very little actual colonization of Africa ever occurred). Borders were drawn based on negotiations which – although they satisfied the demands of European interests – took little thought for the rights and cultures of the various African tribes. As a result, the partition there was great abuse of many of the African people. The partition further created a jigsaw puzzle of land claims that resulted in continuing conflicts and unrest for many African nations.

Colonial regimes also brought with them Christianity. Islam has been in East Africa for many centuries. Human and cattle diseases caused decimation of the black population periodically; "Sufi" teachings were liked by the East Africans as they sought to create a new identity for ex-slaves and women. Colonial economies largely neglected infrastructure needs. They relied on exploiting labor through coercion for agricultural, mineral, explorative or extractive jobs.

After World War I, the Germans were driven out of their colonies by the other colonial powers. During World War II, Africans declared that their loyalty to the Empire would be based on development and democracy. After the war the French started investing in infrastructure in their colonies. In East and Central Africa, whites did not develop the countries. "Smoke in the hills," a typical Tanganyikan rural resistance, slowly spread to all of Peasant Africa. During the 1940's, and 50's development was confined to white sectors only. Anti-colonial nationalism got "majority-rule" regimes to the Congo, Nigeria, Ivory Coast, Senegal, Gabon and Guinea, in 1960 and Sierra Leone, and Tanzania in 1961. Uganda followed in 1962, while Malawi, Kenya and Zambia followed in 1963. Zimbabwe got independence in 1980. The Postcolonial era brought a majority of African countries towards a non-alignment movement – Independent African states, trying to find a way out from the colonial neglect and under-development of many, many decades.

ASIA

The history of building walls as defense is common to many societies throughout the globe. The greatest and most well known of these is the Great Wall of China. Not only is the Great Wall the most extensive fortification ever built, it was a construction that spanned millennia and has come to be a symbol for Chinese nation. Construction on the wall began in the 3rd century BC when Emperor Qin Shui Hang commissioned a vast northern wall in order to keep nomadic barbarians from the north from invading. The structure was originally 3,100 miles long and took 10 years to build. Since that time the wall has been repaired, rebuilt, and extended several times with varying degrees of success. During the Ming Dynasty (after the expulsion of Mongols) it reached a peak of 5,500 miles in length. The most well-preserved and famous portions of the wall are remnants of this period.

Asia consists of East Asia, South East Asia, South Asia and West Asia. In East Asia, South and North Korea, Japan, China, Philippines, Taiwan, etc., are located. Japan is an industrialized nation with a very high per capita income. South Korea is a Newly Industrialized Nation. China is a country aiming to become a Super Power. In South East Asia, Malaysia, Singapore, Indonesia, Brunei, Vietnam, Thailand, Cambodia, Myanmar, etc., are situated.

Starting in the 1960's the economies of several Asian countries began to grow at rapid rates. As a result they have come to be known as the Asian Tigers (or sometimes the Asian Dragons). Specifically the economies of Hong Kong, Singapore, South Korea, and Taiwan grew exponentially from the 1960s to the 1990s. At the beginning of the period, these countries were each considered to be a part of the third world. However, by raising tariffs on imports, capitalizing on their cheap labor force, and focusing on becoming primarily export economies, the Asian Tigers have risen to have some of the highest GDP's in the world. The development of these countries has certainly been unique, but it does have some drawbacks. With such a focus on being an export market, the Tigers are highly dependent on the health of world markets. Despite this, the Asian Tigers have become an inspiration for other developing countries throughout Asia.

South East Asian countries have an economics forum in "ASEAN." South Asia consists of India, Pakistan, Nepal, Bhutan, Bangladesh, Sri Lanka and Maldives. India is an emerging regional power. It has a well-entrenched democratic system. Pakistan has always been under Military Rule, except for a few years of experimentation with a democratic system. Nepal and Bhutan are Monarchies trying to establish a democratic process. Most of the countries are poor. The combined population is huge. India is shaping up as an international hub for information technology.

AUSTRALIA

The commonwealth of Australia had become a Dominion in the year 1901. Most foreign policy matters including offering MFN (Most Favored Nation) status to friendly countries are in the hands of the Imperial power at Britain. Canada, Australia, New Zealand and South Africa are all accorded Dominion status by Britain. The Statute of Westminster, which sought to abrogate the Colonial Laws Validity Act of 1865, in fact ended the superiority of British Parliament over all the four Dominion Parliaments. Australia ratified the statute in 1942. The Great Depression affected Australia greatly. In fact it affected all the four Dominions. All the four Dominions played key roles in establishing of the U.N. (United Nations) at San Francisco. After the 1940's, the four Dominions started dropping the term Dominion from their normal official description.

NORTH AND SOUTH AMERICA

We have studied separately the history of United States. At the beginning of the 20th century, Latin America was composed of 17 sovereign republics plus Cuba and Puerto Rico – two Spanish colonies. They have stable National borders. Most of the countries are rich in minerals. Mexico and Venezuela have petrol and gas, Cuba has sugar, Bolivia has silver and tin, Peru has sugar, copper and cotton and Chile has copper and Nitrates. During 1910-1920, Mexico experienced the greatest social revolution and slowly tilted towards the nationalist-left. After World War I British predominance in Latin America faltered and U.S. business interests prospered, more particularly, in the Caribbean, Middle Americas, Brazil, Peru and Venezuela. The major economies of Latin America embraced industrialization; political thoughts under went a marked change. The U.S. had become the most powerful country, economically, financially, technologically, politically, and militarily.

WORLD HISTORY – POINTS TO REMEMBER

- There were many African uprisings against colonialists. The Menelamba uprising in 1896 of Madagascar, Maji-Maji rising of 1905 in South East Africa, Herrera and Nama rising in South-West Africa in the years 1904-07, Bambatha rising of Zululand in 1905, etc., are important.
- South African Boer War, 1899-1902, was fought by South African British against Afrikaners (Black-African born people).

- The opening up of Katanga copper mine of Northern Rhodesia brought a large labor force and urbanization slowly gained ground.
- 1920's to 1940's saw the African population rising from 140 million to 200 million.
- In 1953, "The Central African Federation of Rhodesia and Nyasaland" was created.
- The Policy of Apartheid was dismantled, and the White-Rule ended on December 22, 1993 when the Parliament approved a Transition Constitution and Nelson Mandela's African National congress won the elections.
- Japan invaded China in 1894 and retained the island of Taiwan as its first overseas colony.
- Japan and Britain signed an alliance in 1902, which gave Japan the courage to attack Russia (in 1904-05 Russo-Japanese War) so as to acquire the southern part of Manchuria.
- China, with the active U.S. investment – U.S. thought to counter Japanese power by encouraging China – started industrialization in a marked manner.
- Japan, owing to domestic polities, signed a number of treaties and agreements at the "Washington Conference 1921-22."
- Japan attacked China in a full-scale war in 1937 in which more than 300,000 ca- sualties were reported on the Chinese side.
- The Indian Empire of the British was a "jewel in the crown" for British as it was twenty times larger than Great Britain itself.
- India was partitioned and both India and partitioned Indian area known as Pakistan got independence from British Rule in 1947 and Ceylon (now Sri Lanka) in the year 1948.
- West Asia has extensive Petroleum resources. Having a centralized voice in OPEC, West Asia is controlling the Petrol prices and is very rich with Petro-Dollars.
- The Whitlam Government in Australia disavowed White-Australia Policy in the year 1974.
- Canada joined NATO in April 1949.
- In early 1990's United States, Canada and Mexico signed "NAFTA" (North American Free Trade Association), an economically strategic agreement just like E.U., making it easier to trade between the three countries.
- Portiro Diaz – Mexico (1876-1911); Estrada Cabrera – Guatemala (1898 – 1920); Cipriano Castro/Juan Vicente Gomez – Venezuela (1899-35) were some of the important Authoritarian Presidents, who did good within their countries.
- 1919, a "red year" in Latin America, on account of wartime inflation inducing labor's militancy.
- Leftists and Jews were hunted down in the streets of Buenos Aires in January 1919 – and that particular week is referred to as the "Tragic Week" in Argentina.

Government & Political Science

Comparative governments refers to the deliberations on studies of various available forms of state systems, how their institutional backdrop or settings were designed and how they perform functionally, what is their constitution like and how it came into being. There are the:

1) Philosophical/Ethical Approach
2) Historical Approach
3) Legal/Judicial Approach
4) Institutional-structural Approach

The first approach was propagated by Plato, Rousseau, Kant, Les Strauses, Hagel et al. in which a study of the state and its institutions is invariably linked to the moral, ethical and high principles involved in government and people. The Historical Approach was propagated by A.J. Carlyle, Catlin, Dunning, McIlwain and G.H. Sabine. To understand the Governmental Institutions and processes, this theory states, a clear understanding of the historical background is necessary.

The legal/judicial approach was propounded by Austin, Bentham, Jean Bodin, A.V. Dicey and Hobbes. According to this theory the study of comparative governments is interlinked with the study of legal and judicial aspects of the state.

The Institution-Structural approach was propounded by Bagehot, James Bryce, Giovanni Sartori et al. This approach wants the scope of comparative Governments to be limited to the Constitutional provisions of the formal institutions like the Executive, the Legislature and the Judiciary. Comparative analysis of such institutions is a must under this theory. All the above four approaches are called Traditional Approaches.

The Modern Approaches are:

1) The Behavioral Approach
2) System Analysis Approach

The Behavioral Approach:

- Focuses attention on the "Individual" and "Group" behavior and on political processes
- They spell out new methods and insist upon survey research
- They borrow from the various disciplines of social and natural science

The protagonists of this theory are: Almond, Robert Dahl, David Easton, Heinz Eulan, Lasswell and Charles Merriam.

The system analysis approach relies on input-out and structural functional approach. They try to know:

- the function of the political system as such
- the structure of the political system
- the conditions under which the system works best

The protagonists are David Easton and Almond. In addition to the Traditional and Modern Approach, there is one more approach, which is basically different from both, and that is the Marxist Approach.

Although there are as many different forms of government as there are nations, governmental systems can be divided into two broad groups: authoritarian and democratic. Democratic governments are governments that are focused on the individuals in a society. In a purely democratic society, every individual's opinion would be given weight in any matter to be decided on. Any form of representative government or government characterized by voting would fall into this category.

In contrast, authoritarian governments have a stronger focus on the centralization of power. The rights and powers of individuals are largely overlooked. Examples of authoritarian governments include totalitarian regimes, military governments, socialist governments, and monarchies.

The sharp difference between authoritative and democratic governments can be demonstrated by the two Greek city states of Athens and Sparta. In Athens the citizens were all considered equal before the law. Education was highly valued, and citizens were directly involved in electing leaders to fill governmental roles. All of this has allowed Athens to be remembered as a bright example of a democratic society. On the other hand, citizens of Sparta were sharply divided in class roles. Men, women, and a class of slaves were separated and trained in their specific roles. The city-state was ruled by two kings and a group of elders who made all decisions. In contrast to the democratic society of Athens, Spartan government was highly militaristic and authoritative.

EXECUTIVE, LEGISLATIVE AND JUDICIARY

The U.S. has time-tested governing institutions in the Executive, the Legislative and the Judiciary. The enforcement division of the government, both federal and state, functions exceptionally well and the U.S. stands tall for all other democracies and aspiring democracies. Democracy is identified with liberalism. The liberal state, by extension, is a mélange of free market economy and the principles of universal adult franchise. In representative democracy people have a right to choose their representatives through periodic elections conducted on the basis of universal adult franchise. The age for participating in such elections vary from country to country, normally from 18 to 21 years.

In countries like the Netherlands and Belgium; citizens are compelled by law to vote in the General Elections. Rights have corresponding duties and obligations. "He who takes, gives and he who gives, takes" is how a society works. International Relations refer to the dynamics of interaction between countries of the world. Here, trust, security and defense, dominance, retaliatory qualities, sense of accommodation, reciprocity as well as vigilance are taken into consideration during interaction. Commerce has now become a forceful interactive instrument in today's international relations.

UNITED NATIONS

The United Nations is an international organization founded in 1945 after the Second World War by 51 countries committed to maintaining international peace and security, developing friendly relations among nations and promoting social progress, better living standards and human rights.

The United Nations has four main purposes:

- To keep peace throughout the world;
- To develop friendly relations among nations;
- To help nations work together to improve the lives of poor people, to conquer hunger, disease and illiteracy, and to encourage respect for each other's rights and freedoms;
- To be a centre for harmonizing the actions of nations to achieve these goals.

The constitution provides certain rights and priviledges to its citizens. This also ensures the right of **habeas corpus**, which means the individual who is accused must appear in court and must know the charges against him or her.

STATELESS NATION

The Kurds are a people who inhabit the mountainous regions where Turkey, Iran, and Iraq meet. Although Kurdistan existed as an independent nation from 1920-1923, it has not existed as an independent state since then, and as a result is considered to be the world's largest stateless nation.

In other words, although the Kurdish people possess a distinct culture, language, centralized location and ethnicity, they are citizens of several nations without one to call their own. The Kurdish people speak the Kurdish language which is similar to Farsi and takes many words from Arabic, and the majority of the people ascribe to some form of Islam. Despite their continuing desire for independence, the people remain under the control of various Middle-Eastern countries, with a majority of the Kurdish people living in Turkey.

MCCULLOCH V. MARYLAND

The case of McCulloch v. Maryland was a significant court case in the United States because of its impact in shaping the powers of the still-developing federal government. In 1816, the Second Bank of the United States was established in Maryland due to an act by Congress. Although it was technically a public bank, it was responsible for handling all transaction of the federal government and answered to both The U.S. Treasury and Congress.

Two years later, the state of Maryland imposed a law which required all banks that were not state-chartered (which included the Second Bank of the United States) to pay certain taxes to the state of Maryland. When the head of the bank, James McCulloch, refused to pay the tax, he was sued by the state. Although the Maryland state courts initially found in favor of the state, the Supreme Court overturned the ruling.

This case became significant because it not only established the federal government's right to establish and charter banks, but also implied that state governments have no power to interfere with acts of Congress. In other words, it firmly established the supremacy of the federal government, and expanded the rights of the federal government beyond those specifically given in the Constitution.

MARBURY V. MADISON

As President John Adam's presidency came to a close, he issued several appointments on his last night as president. Among these was an appointment to William Marbury as justice of the peace in the District of Columbia. However, due to the lateness of his appointment, the appointment was never made official and when Thomas Jefferson took office, his Secretary of State James Madison did not honor the appointment. Marbury took the matter to court and asked for a writ of mandamus (an order from the court to a government official that requires them to fulfill their duty) that would allow him to take his position as justice of the peace. The right to issue such a writ of mandamus had been granted to the courts in the Judiciary Act of 1789.

In a unanimous decision, the court ruled that Marbury and the others did in fact have a right to their positions. However, the court stated that they did not have a right to issue the writ of mandamus because that provision in the Judiciary Act of 1789 was unconstitutional. By this, the courts denied themselves a small right (to issue the writ of mandamus), but seized a much greater power: the power of constitutional review. This was the first case in which the Supreme Court stated their right to declare an act of the legislature to be unconstitutional, and it established the power of judicial review that is still in effect today.

LEGISLATIVE POWERS

All legislative powers in the United States are granted to the two houses of Congress by the Constitution. Although bills originate in the House of Representatives, both houses have a say. In order for a Bill to be passed into law, it must be passed by simple majority in both the Senate and the House of Representatives.

If the two houses pass a particular bill in different forms, then a committee comprising members of both houses is created to reconcile the two bills and it must again pass through both the House of Representatives and the Senate in order to become law.

Because the Senate always has an even number of members, there is potential for the vote to be an exact tie. If this is the case then the right is given to the Vice President of the United States (who is considered to be the President of the Senate) to break the tie.

FREEDOM OF THE PRESS

John Peter Zenger was a German immigrant to America, and one of the few skilled publishers in the New York area. He worked editing and printing a newspaper called the New York Weekly Journal. It was one of two newspapers in the area at the time, and the only one that dared print criticisms of officials appointed by the British monarchy. When Zenger allowed an article critical of Governor Crosby (governor of New York at the time) he was charged with libel.

At the time, a person could be convicted of libel any time they published criticisms of the government. After seven months in jail his case was finally brought to trial and he was defended by Alexander Hamilton – a popular lawyer and public figure. In defense of Zenger, Hamilton claimed that a man could not be convicted of libel if he published the truth. Although the judge ordered the jury to convict Zenger based on whether or not he had printed the article, the verdict came back as a unanimous "not guilty." Although true freedom of press was not established until the Bill of Rights, this case was a major milestone for the creation of free press in America.

Sociology

The scientific study of societies and the behavior of people in groups is referred to as sociology. Human beings are known to be gregarious. They love company, social interactions. The development of human beings from infant to child to adult to ripe old age requires social ties, backing, sympathy, empathy, and encouragement of family and society. Society as a whole has a bearing on our development. Sociology seeks to study both intensively and extensively such social relationships vis-à-vis an individual member of a given society.

DEMOGRAPHY, DEVIANCE, FAMILY INTERACTION, METHODS, ETC.
Demography encompasses the study of how human populations tend to change. It deals with the study of birth and death, marriages, divorces, etc., happening in a particular region or area and at a particular time.

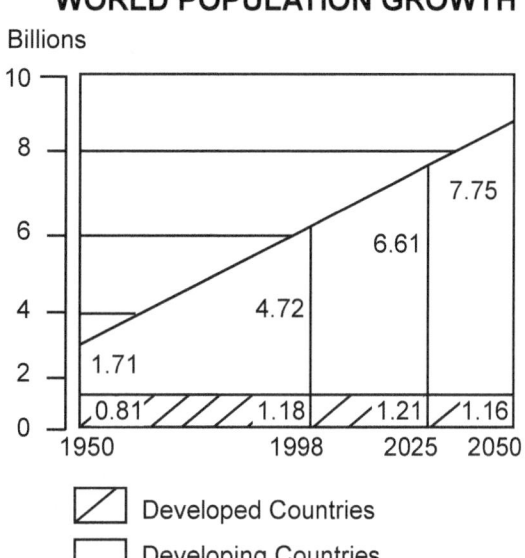

Demographic Transition relates to the changes in population associated with economic development. There are 3-Phases involved in a demographic transition model.

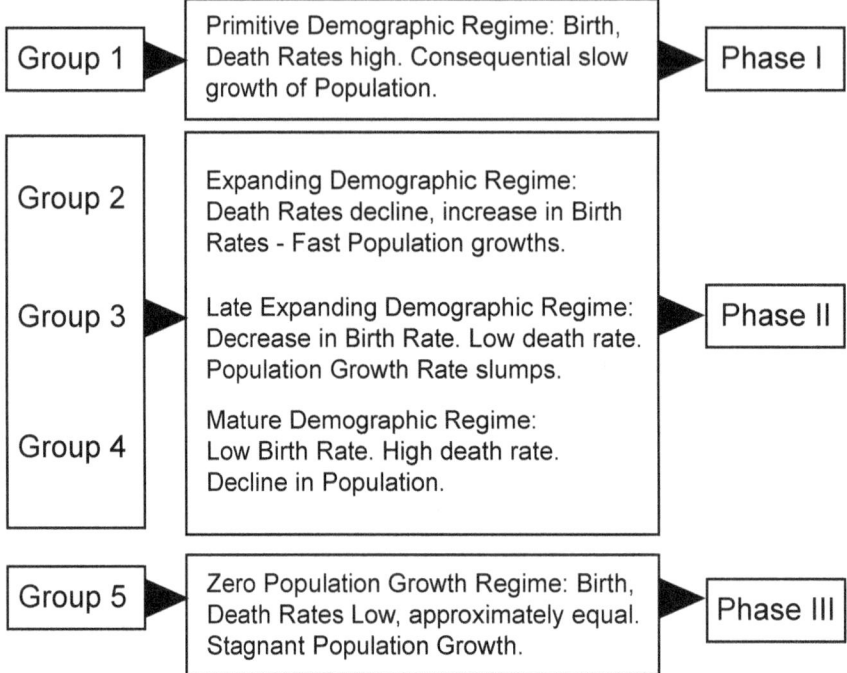

Demographics

Demographics are the way that marketers and researchers classify people. Example of demographics are age, sex, race, religion, nationality, country of origin, income, marital status, etc. A demographic is anything that can group you into a category with other people.

Deviance

It means different, mostly in a bad way, from what is considered normal or acceptable. The behavior pattern of deviant characters tells us a story of abnormality tinged with a criminal bent of mind. Criminals, murderers and terrorists are all known to possess an abnormal, almost sadistic and highly perverted mental makeup, which aims always at distractive behavior.

Family

A family is a group of people who are related to each other by blood, like father, mother and their offspring. Children are born and brought up by individuals' families and, naturally, they are conditioned to uphold whatever may be the perceived family traditions, cultures and value systems. In a child's development, the basic value system comes from the family. A child is not encouraged to think outside the traditional family values. A family plays a very important role in shaping up a child's attitudes and behavior patterns. Parental expectations, if encouraging and supportive without fear of punishment, lead a child to achieve even tougher goals. Consistent punishment will lead to fixative behavior. It is the family that is at the root of a child developing into a normal child or a deviant one.

Interaction

What is interaction? It is the activity of talking to, or working together with other people. Human beings do not inherit any given behavior trait, but, a tendency to behave in a particular way that becomes predominantly expressed in one way in a particular situation and differently in another situation. It may also remain unexpressed but latent in another situation. This condition is known as the "interaction principle."

ASCRIBED AND ACHIEVED STATUS

In sociology the description of status – or the different roles and positions that a person occupies in a social structure – is an important element in understanding behavior. There are two main types of statuses: ascribed and achieved.

An ascribed status is a status that an individual doesn't have any control over. For example, race, ethnicity, where a person falls in his or her family, or the presence genetic conditions would all be ascribed statuses. often ascribed statuses are conditions that a person is born with, but it can also be something that they just have no control over. For example, children rarely have any control over their living environment. That comes as a result of decisions made by parents and is therefore an ascribed status for them.

In contrast to ascribed statuses are achieved statuses. These are aspects of an individual's life that they do control. Ascribed statuses are determined by a individual's own actions and merit. For example, the status of college graduate, CEO, parent, thief, and doctor are all a result of conscious decisions and effort on the part of the individual. Ascribed and achieved statuses are not necessarily mutually exclusive, and often overlap. While living situation is an ascribed status for the child, it is an achieved status for the parents. This means that the same situation can be classified differently based on perspective.

RESEARCH

To study the way that people grow, learn, adapt and interact with others, psychologists use a standardized method so that other people in the scientific community can understand their findings and agree on research.

Scientists use a specific vocabulary to conduct their research. A **participant** is a person that a scientist studies in their experiment. They can also be referred to as a subject. When a scientist is performing an experiment on an animal, they are also referred to as a subject or a participant.

When scientists want to study an entire city, culture, or population, they will use a sample. A **sample** is a small collection of subjects. The number of people you need to participate to make the sample the most accurate is statistically generated based on the amount of the population.

Everything that a scientist measures and studies is called a **variable**. For example, if you were conducting research on insomnia, you would have variables which include the amount of time it takes a person to fall asleep, how much caffeine they ingest, how much alcohol or drugs they ingest, what distractions are in the room, etc.

Research must meet four main tests:

1. Research must be **replicable**. Another scientist, given the information regarding the experiment, should be able to reproduce the experiment with the same results. This is how the scientific community accepts or rejects new theories. If the experiment can be reproduced several times by different people in different organizations or locations, it lends to its credibility. This means that the theory must be quantitative, or measurable and not qualitative. Qualitative means that some- thing is similar in structure or organization but it cannot be measured in numerical terms.
2. The research must be **falsifiable**. This means that a theory has to be stated in a way that can be rejected or accepted. Think of it as asking a yes or no question. Is smoking bad for you? The answer is yes or no, and can be proven. This could be stated as "smoking is bad for you because it contains carcinogens." This is a falsifiable statement. It needs to be stated this way so that it can be proved or disproved. If a researcher does not consider all the evidence, but ignores the infor- mation that does not prove their theory and accepts the information that proves it, they are showing **confirmation bias**.
3. The research must be precisely stated and conducted. A theory needs to be stated precisely so it can be replicated. Scientists use operational definitions to state exactly how a variable will be measured. For example, a researcher studying birth order may notice that children who are the oldest of several siblings tend to be more responsible as adults and parents. The researcher may conclude that this is because they have experienced more time nurturing and caring for younger siblings. In our birth order study, the scientist needs to find a way to measure responsible. He or she might decide that they will use the individual's credit reports as an operational variable to show responsibility.

4. Researchers must use the most logical, simplest explanation possible as an answer to their theory. This is also called the **principle of parsimony** or **Occam's razor.**

EXPERIMENTS

In experiments, a researcher manipulates variables to test theories and conclusions. Each experiment has independent and dependent variables. This is how researchers test cause and effect links and relationships.

The independent variable is the variable that researchers have direct control over. The dependent variable is then observed by the researcher.

In experiments, there are usually two groups of participants. One group is the experimental group and one group is the control group. The most common example is in medical trials. Let's say there is a trial run of a new diet drug. The researcher will split the group randomly in two. Group 1 will receive the diet pill that is being tested. Group 2 will receive a placebo pill. The placebo pill is simply a sugar pill. Group 2 will not know that they are not receiving the real drug. This allows the researchers to study the true effectiveness and side-effects of the pill. When the people are assigned to a group randomly, it is called **random assignment**. This particular experiment was a single-blind experiment. A **double-blind** experiment is when none of the doctors, researches and participants know who is getting the real drug. It is assigned by computer or an independent individual where it is kept confidential until the conclusion of the study.

SOCIAL CHANGE, SOCIAL ORGANIZATION, SOCIAL STRATIFICATION AND SOCIAL THEORY

Social changes occur periodically. The way of life of people was not the same after the Agricultural Revolution and then Industrial Revolution. We are now in the midst of an Information Technology Revolution, which is changing our way of life. We are living in the knowledge – economy. Lifestyle of people has changed and today's fast-lane work ethic has brought in its wake fast-food culture! People prefer a restaurant to cooking at home.

Change is the essence of life and social changes are even more so. Any given social group may be described as a special type of social organization. They interact individually in order to achieve a collective goal. Members of such social organizations have definite roles. Entering the organization or, for that matter, leaving it, is regulated by policies and rules. Individual goals are satisfied by achieving collective goals. Leadership is well defined and followers are bound by the actions of leaders. Social organization is a collective mind programmed to achieve for the members of that social group their collective goals. All social systems are basically class-oriented, i.e., the materials and other cultural inputs are dispersed in an unequal manner. Marx's famous "working class" is again stratified into skilled, semi-skilled, and unskilled. Middle class is again divided into white-collar, blue-collar and non-manual workers. Rigid class relations are created and maintained by hierarchies.

Marx says: "…The ideas of the ruling class are in every epoch the ruling ideas: i.e., the class which is the ruling material force of society is at the same time its ruling intellectual force. The class which has the means of material production at its disposal, has control at the same time over the means of mental production, so that thereby, generally speaking, the ideas of those who lack the means of mental production are subject to it…"

Again, M. Weber, "Economy and Society" states about class: "…Ownership of dwellings; workshops; warehouses; stores; agriculturally usable land in large or small holdings – a quantitative difference with possibly qualitative consequences; ownership with mines; cattle; men (slaves); disposition over mobile instruments of production, or capital goods of all sorts, especially money or objects that can easily be exchanged for money; disposition over products of one's own labor or of others' labor differing according to their various distances from consumability; disposition over transferable monopolies of any kind – all these distinctions differentiate the class situations of the propertied…"

In today's knowledge-economy, unskilled workers are very minimal. However, it also brought a digital divide – the class that has knowledge and access to computers and Internet on the one hand and the class which does not have access to computers. These can be referred to as the have and have nots.

What is a theory? A theory is an idea or set of ideas that is intended to explain something about life or the world, especially one that has not been proven to be true. Karl Marx felt that society should be studied in a critical way aiming at structural reform. Ulrich Beck's concept of "Risk society" theory in its essence is a broad analysis of modernization. With the failure of communism, Marxism has lost its validity. In today's context, a theory of society should largely orient itself with the creation of not a Utopian society, but, a just, meaningful and humane society.

C. WRIGHT MILLS

In 1956, Charles Wright Mills wrote his book *The Power Elite*, in which he discussed his power elite theory. The power elite theory divides the population into three groups, which can be organized into a sort of pyramid. The smallest and highest level, the power elite, is a small group of people who regularly decide the most important decisions for the whole country, as opposed to multiple groups who all work together to make decisions. The middle level deals with relatively minor issues, and the masses have no decision making power at all. For example, the President of the United States and his closest advisors and cabinet members would be members of the power elite, along with the most influential members of the legislature and the Supreme Court.

Mills was also very concerned about what he considered to be the loss of a middle class. He placed a significant importance on knowledge as a means of bringing about change, and felt that knowledge could be obtained through critical thinking.

In his book *The Sociological Imagination*, Mills identifies biography, social structure, and history as three elements of "Sociological Imagination" which allows an individual to look beyond their personal environment and concerns to see the bigger picture of the society and enable themselves to find solutions. Essentially, sociological imagination is the ability to apply the concepts of sociology into life by viewing events objectively rather than seeing only the individual perspective. Using such a perspective, events can be considered in terms of how an individual circumstance influences societal norms, and how society norms will influence that circumstance. Thus, a greater understanding can be reached by considering situations more holistically.

FRANCES PERKINS

Frances Perkins was born Fannie Perkins in April of 1880 in Boston. Her parents ensured that she received a good education from a young age, and encouraged her to attend college. She was very intelligent and popular – even becoming class president. Despite her parent's expectation that she would take a teaching position and wait for a suitable marriage prospect, Frances had a strong desire to improve the world of working women and children.

She instead searched for positions in social work. From very early in her career, Perkins was a strong advocate of the rights of women and children in the workplace. For her, the 1911 fire at the Triangle Shirtwaist Factory, which was responsible for the deaths of nearly 200 women, was the last straw. She rededicated herself to bring about a change.

In 1929 she was appointed by Theodore Roosevelt (then governor of New York) as the Industrial Commissioner of the State of New York. She worked closely with him and when the stock market crashed and spurred the Great Depression, she urged him to do something about unemployment. She traveled abroad studying different systems and seeking solutions to implement in New York.

When Roosevelt was elected president in 1932 he appointed Perkins as his Secretary of Labor. Throughout his presidency Perkins was a critical supporter of "New Deal" programs that would bring reform to the workplace. She was instrumental in the development of Social Security and the Fair Labor Standards Act. Perkins served throughout Roosevelt's presidency, and at the time of his death was the longest serving labor secretary.

Economics

Economics is the art of making choices in the presence of scarcity and choice. In other words, economics is all about scarcity and choice. If there is no scarcity of resources, i.e., if goods are available without any restrictions and in plenty, the act of choosing becomes needless. Water is available in plenty (at least in most of the countries) and therefore presents no choice – likewise air. Economics deals mainly with scarcity and seeks to study alternative choices. In doing so, theories, principles, and practices are developed for future applications.

Capitalism is a monetary and social system where individuals are encouraged to make new businesses and work for as great of a profit as they can. The United States is a capitalistic society. In a capitalistic society, the government has limited influence in private business although they do enforce some business laws and practices.

Socialism is a system where the good of the group supercedes the good of the private individual. Each person works for bettering society as whole. The government controls almost all natural resources, business and social programs.

In welfare capitalism, the government pays for all education and health coverage. It is a market based system as well. Sweden and Canada are examples of welfare capitalism.

Communism is when the means of production are owned equally and the profits are shared equally. Although it has been attempted many times to create a utopia of sorts based on communism, it is considered a flawed system. The book "Animal Farm" is a wonderful analogy to the social systems, particularly communism.

KEYNESIAN ECONOMICS

Traditionally there have been two overarching schools of thought that have dominated beliefs about economic systems: Austrian and Keynesian. The Austrian school of thought goes back to Adam Smith's book *The Wealth of Nations* in which he argues that economies are naturally self-regulating and self-repairing. As a result, when tough economic times hit, the only sensible thing to do is to wait and watch as an "invisible hand" pushes the economy back to normal.

For over a century this belief dominated academic thought. However, with the onset of the Great Depression in the early 1900s, John Maynard Keynes sought to explain the severity of the depression and proposed his own theory as a more viable solution to the economic downturn. Keynes argued that the Austrian opinion was flawed because it made the assumption that people would be willing to spend excess money that they had. Keynes disagreed and stated that in difficult economic times people were far less likely to spend excess money. Rather, they would hoard it and this fact would prevent the economy from fixing itself.

To solve this conundrum, Keynes proposed that rather than simply waiting for things to get better it was vital for the government to take action. He proposed in such situations the government should establish a practice of high spending and low taxes in order to offset low consumer spending. This would create a deficit in the federal budget, but would ultimately spur the economy back to normal. Then, when the economy was again fully functioning, the federal government simply needed to reverse the trend by increasing taxes and lowering spending. By so doing, it could create a surplus and pay down any debts incurred during the depression period.

Ever since the time of the Great Depression, the United States government has undoubtedly leaned towards Keynesian policy. Time has proven several difficulties with this theory, however. During times of economic downturn, everyone is happy to have lowered taxes and high government spending. The trouble comes when it is time to unwind the pattern. There is a possibility that reversing spending can simply plunge the economy into another downturn, and furthermore it is often a politically disastrous move. There are several merits to the Keynesian theory, and time will tell how it plays out in its entirety.

SCARCITY, CHOICE, COST, ECONOMICS MEASUREMENT

Resources are limited. How to choose, then, between competing needs? Well, let us assume that country "A" has a choice either to produce automobiles or wheat for consumption. What are the production choice possibilities? Let us study:

It can be graphically represented as:

CHOICES	AUTOMOBILES (In Millions)	WHEAT (In Millions Lbs)
A	0	15
B	1	14
C	2	12
D	3	9
E	4	5
F	5	0

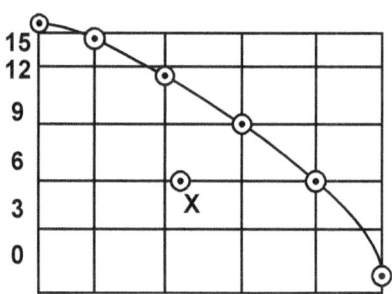

This graph shows us other things being equal, the choice a society has to make between producing wheat or automobiles. The point "X" in the middle shows us that the resources are not being utilized in the best possible way. Since production of scarce resources to suit the needs of a given society at a given time period is central to economic studies, cost of production assumes significance. Fixed costs are those which are independent of the level of input. Whether you produce 7000 numbers or 5000 numbers, fixed costs are bound to be the same. On the other side of the spectrum you have variable costs which vary according to the level of inputs. Overhead costs may be defined as the costs that are independent of the level of output.

There is another cost, the marginal cost. If there is an increase in the total costs or total variable costs incurred on account of producing an additional unit of goods it is known as marginal cost. You get the average cost of production of a given by dividing the total cost with the output turned out. In a market, if there is only one seller in a market, it is known as monopoly. What he charges is the price! A monopolistic competition, on the other hand, is a market in which there are a large number of sellers. They produce differentiated products and there is free entry and exit to the markets. Product markets are markets where products needed by the consumers are marketed. Consumable goods, durable goods, non-durable goods, semi-durable goods, perishable goods – all these goods are needed by consumers. Goods that are required for further production of other goods are known as producer's goods or capital goods.

MONETARY AND FISCAL POLICY

Monetary and fiscal policies are the instruments in the hands of governments all over the world to control inflation, economic growth – stagnation as well as unemployment. Monetary and credit policies are spelled out by the central bank which is considered the banker of bankers, of course in consultation with the government of the day. A government which follows a well-thought-out fiscal policy by varying the public expenditure and tax totals can produce a balanced budget, which is healthy. If, in the process, they obtain a deficit or surplus, it is bound to impact the level of prices, money and real incomes, unemployment and total production. A fiscal policy, which is considered not good or bad, can impact the business cycles adversely. A mature and well-stabilized fiscal policy can have a moderating effect on the up swings and down swings of business.

BUDGET DEFICITS

Anytime a government's expenditures exceed its tax revenue this creates a budget deficit. In other words, a budget deficit is when a government is spending more than it is making. Although many economists argue that in times of economic recession this can stimulate the economy, as a consistent practice deficit spending is fatal to an economy and to the integrity of a government.

When there is a consistent pattern of deficit spending it is called a structural deficit. This indicates that there is something structurally or fundamentally wrong with the system that prevents the government from achieving a balanced budget. If there is a pattern of alternating budget deficit and budget surplus (when the tax revenues exceed spending and there is extra money) this is called a cyclical deficit.

A cyclical deficit does not necessarily indicate a major budget problem, because over the aggregate of the cycle, the budget does balance. In any case, whenever there is a budget deficit, the remaining funds are obtained through the issuance of bonds. A bond is essentially a short term loan in which the issuer (the government) promises to repay a certain amount of money at a certain time in the future. In the United States, government bonds offer lengths varying from 1 month to 30 years. Theoretically, bonds are issued in a period of deficit, and paid back in a time of surplus.

INTERNATIONAL TRADE

What is international trade? It deals with an exchange of goods and services among countries of the world. Some countries have the expertise and skill required to produce a particular set of goods most efficiently. Still others have expertise and skill to produce yet another set of goods most efficiently. By using this comparative advantage, a country which is good at producing a particular set of products most efficiently exchanges that set of goods with the other country, which is good at producing efficiently another set of products. Both the countries are profited by this method. Factor endowment theory emphasizes differences in relative factor endowments as the basis of comparative advantage and trade. Hi-tech machineries are being produced by the United States most efficiently and effectively. There is a comparative advantage, say, with India. India, on the other hand, has comparative advantages over products and services in the area of information technology. It is profitable for both the United States and India to exchange hi-tech machinery with information technology products and services respectively. This is the basic thinking in international trade.

As the year 1900 approached, the United States was becoming more and more established as a world power. However, still being a fairly young country, it was disadvantaged in matters of international trade. of particular concern to many was the difficulty of trading with China. Despite earlier agreements of free trade in Asia, many European countries had begun establishing spheres of influence where they held powerful trade advantages in China.

Fearing the disadvantage that this could bring, Secretary of State John Hay took action by circulating "Open Door Notes." In these notes, he proposed an international agreement involving Japan, France, Britain, Russia, and others involved in heavy trade in China. The idea was to establish an "Open Door Policy" that would allow fair trade. Essentially, the agreement would forbid favoritism or discrimination in trade based on nationality. Most of the powers agreed to the proposal based on its practicality, and those who may have disagreed with it were not willing to challenge the consensus. The Open Door Policy moved forward, and the sovereignty of China was preserved.

ECONOMICS – POINTS TO REMEMBER

- Break-even-analysis refers to the price at which firms make zero-profit. To put it in another way, Break-even-price is exactly equal to the average cost.
- Constant returns to scale presents when a proportionate increase in all inputs leads to the similar proportionate increase in the output.
- Decreasing/diminishing returns to scale presents when a proportionate increase in all inputs produces an output which is less than a proportionate increase of inputs.
- Elasticity of demand-refers to a situation where the price elasticity of demand-is greater than unity (i.e., one).
- In Elastic demand – refers to a situation where the price elasticity of demand is less than unity.
- Labor coefficient is equal to the units of labor needed to make a single unit of output.
- Increasing return to scale presents when a proportionate increase in all inputs cre- ates a more than proportionate rise in the outputs.
- Returns to scale refer to the effect of a proportionate gain in all inputs vis-à-vis outputs.
- Law of demand refers to a situation where any given rise in the price of a product pulls down the quantity demanded.
- Law of supply is an increase in the price of any goods lead to a rise in the quantity supplied.
- Marginal revenue refers to the rise in total revenue when an additional unit is sold.

Introduction to Psychology

When people think and behave under normal conditions – this is the basic premise of psychology. Social psychology deals with the social side of an individual's thoughts and actions. Physiological psychology deals with an individual's thoughts and actions at the neural level. Comparative psychology deals with an individual's thoughts and actions compared to other species on earth. The thoughts and behavior patterns of children as they grow, is the foundation of child psychology. Any particular thought and action of an individual is the subject matter of abnormal psychology.

AGGRESSION

The behavior of an individual is always goal-oriented. The basic unit of any behavior is an activity. Motives are considered the "Whys" of behavior. Motives are interchanged with wants, needs, impulses or drives within an individual.

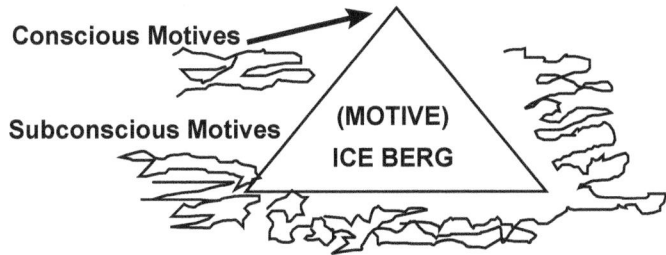

According to Sigmund Freud, motives are like an iceberg. Your conscious motives are akin to the tip and the subconscious motives are the submerged portions of an iceberg. If a need or motive is satisfied, it does not remain a motive any more. If a need is blocked or, thwarted, frustration sets in. This may lend to irrational behavior, which may include aggression, rationalization, regression, fixation or resignation. Aggression is mostly likely to lead towards behaviors which are destructive. Open hostility or even resorting to physical abuse are common forms of destructive behavior. Rationalization is finding excuses. Regression is childish behavior. Fixation is continuing the same behavior pattern even though you know you have been punished many times for that behavior. Resignation is tepid acceptance of whatever happens.

Sigmund Freud's analysis of human personality and subconscious drives features three main components - id, ego, and superego. Together, these mechanisms combine to aide us in our decision-making and guide us to become the unique individuals that we all are. Robert Young, a professor with expertise in this area, provided the following information used to understand the id, superego and the ego.

The id contains the psychic content related to the primitive instincts of the body, notably sex and aggression, as well as all psychic material that is inherited and present at birth. It functions entirely according to the pleasure-pain principle, its impulses either seeking immediate fulfillment or settling for a compromise fulfillment.

The superego is the ethical component of the personality and provides the moral standards by which the ego operates.

The ego coexists, in psychoanalytic theory; with the id and superego...it is the integrator between the outer and inner worlds, as well as between the id and the superego. The ego gives continuity and consistency to behavior by providing a personal point of reference, which relates the events of the past (retained in memory) and actions of the present and of the future (represented in anticipation and imagination).

The main trio of characters found in Star Trek, the original series -- McCoy, Kirk, and Spock -- makes for an interesting analogy of human personality as they each show characteristics of Freud's concepts of the id, ego, and superego. Hopefully, this analogy will make it easier for you to understand and remember this theory.

THE ID - James T. Kirk, always enjoyed a good fight, risked his ship and crew often, and always fed his libido with an assortment of females. *Kirk*, with his passion for gratification in terms of aggression and sex, displays characteristics of the id.

THE SUPEREGO - Doctor Leonard (Bones) McCoy, always reminded his Captain of the rules and morality of any situation. He also is known for his arguments with Spock, just as the superego and ego are often in conflict.

THE EGO - Mr. Spock was the bringer of balance between the impulses of the id and the extreme caution of the superego by his use of logic and understanding of his Captain's needs as well as understanding the morality base of Bones. While Spock and Bones were often at odds, they always worked toward the same end -- a correct and feasible solution to any given situation.

Together - Kirk, McCoy, and Spock represent the triadic conflict within all humans, thus the three distinct characters, taken together, form an understanding of the human condition.[1]

CONFORMITY

To put it simply, conformity is consciously or sub-consciously keeping one's behavior pattern in line with that of the group. This is a known phenomenon evident throughout history. By so doing, one avoids conflict with the group behavior.

GROUP PROCESS METHODS

In a group, each member has a formal role. In other words, each group member is expected to exhibit a pattern of behavior in conformity with the group behavior. A role is always associated with a certain standing, or, shall we say, status in the group. A group consists of many members each having a formal role, but often the roles of group members are complementary. In addition to a formal role, a group member may also have developed an informal role. In everyday life, we not only assume many roles but also become expert in switching from one to the other with relative ease.

In the animal world animals don't have roles, status, titles or positions. They are guided by raw power – strength. Brutal strength determines the leader of a given group. In a human group, roles, status, etc., are determined basically by one's erudition, money-power and of course intelligence.

A leader has a fairly explicit Role. Leadership abilities require adjusting capabilities to different situations. The leadership style of a person is the behavior pattern that individual reveals when attempting to influence the actions of others as perceived by those others. A relationship-oriented leader scores over a task-oriented leader, in most cases. But, again, this varies from situation to situation.

PERFORMANCE

There is a distinction between learning and performance. One can learn by simply observing. Here one acquires a behavior, without any practice. It is not trial learning. The act of doing any given task is performance. Performance requires practice. For a performance to be effective, one has to put in additional inputs in the form of appropriate reinforcements. A highly motivated person's performance may increase to 80 to 90% of that person's ability.

PERSONALITY

According to Sigmund Freud's **Theory of Psychoanalysis**, the personality of a person is deeply influenced by two basic forces, aggression and sex drive. These forces are inborn and cannot be driven away. Another school of thought persists that individuals differ markedly from one another even though they behave most consistently in a number of situations. A trait is a persistent tendency and a person's personality is made up of these traits. According to operant learning theory, personality is composed of reinforced responses, attained via environmental forces. The Humanistic viewpoint emphasizes that all people are inherently good.

SOCIALIZATION

Socialization can be summed up as the way an individual behaves in a cultural and social backdrop. It deals with the society, individual interactions and impacts attitudes, personality and motivations. Human beings are basically social animals. They need constant company. Social behavior depends mostly on the culture to which one belongs. A newborn baby slowly learns to interact with parents, other siblings, and other children. This interaction grows with age and still greater socialization is achieved. Interpersonal attraction is influenced by a variety of factors, like personality, appearance, intelligence, and similarity of interests and close proximity. Conformity plays a significant role in group socialization. The general tendency of a group member is to conform to group norms even though the member is aware that the facts are totally against such norms. In the process of socialization, mass media today has acquired a unique persuasive role.

INTRODUCTION TO PSYCHOLOGY – POINTS TO REMEMBER

- An attempt to overcome impediments by trial-and-error problem solving is known as "coping behavior."
- If motives are blocked, or, if there is a continuous failure of rational coping behavior, irrational coping behavior is resorted to.
- Dissonance occurs when two perceptions that are relevant to each other are in conflict.
- The blocking or stopping of goal achievement is known as frustration.
- Availability is the perceived limitations of the environment.
- The perceived probability of fulfillment of a given need of an individual based on previous experience is known as expectancy.
- As an individual grows, he develops conditioned responses, i.e., habit patterns, to different stimuli, and the sum total of such habit patterns, as perceived by others, builds his personality.
- The inborn physical drives of human beings are referred to as the id.
- As part of personality development, a child learns and becomes aware of sex roles, which impacts the child to take more interest in parent of the opposite sex. In a boy it is known as the Oedipus complex, and in girls it is referred to as the Electra complex.
- If an individual is out of contact with reality, he is referred to as psychotic.
- Abundant irrational thought leads to a form of Psychosis known as Schizophrenia.
- Three "Soma" (body) types: 1. Endomorphic – Prominent belly and fatness (A 'sumo' wrestler) 2. Mesomorphic – Muscle built body. 3. Ectomorphic – lean looking with no flesh whatsoever. "Vicerotonic" revels in eating, as he is Endomorphic. "Somatotonic" revels in bodybuilding and is energetic as he is mesomorphic. "Cerebrotonic" revels in thinking; he is lean as he is an ectomorphic.

- Psychoanalysis attempts to trace any childhood conflict that is deeply embedded in the sub-conscious with a view to cure the patient of the difficult childhood ex- periences.

MEMORY

Memory is often associated with an ability to recall facts for a test or names of new acquaintances. The effects of memory, however, reach much farther than simple recall of facts or figures. Memory plays an essential role in every person's life, and decisions are made constantly that rely on information found in memory. There are three overarching categories of memory: sensory memory, short-term memory, and long-term memory. Each type of memory has a different span and function.

Sensory memory has the shortest span which is typically less than one second and processes the greatest amount of information. It holds the record of all events relating to the five senses. The brightness of light in a room, the pitch, tone, and volume of various noises, and the textures of items in a surrounding are all examples of details processed by sensory memory. Unless a person makes a conscious decision to focus on an aspect of these memories, they are discarded immediately. For example, most people are not constantly aware of the feel of clothing on their skin or the quiet hum of an air conditioner unless they have a specific reason to be aware of it.

The second category of memory, short-term memory, has a slightly longer span of closer to one minute. Short-term memory is also known as working memory because these are the things that an individual is actively focusing on. This stage of memory is associated with remembering and processing information. Once the information is no longer actively needed it begins to fade. Only a small amount of information can be in short-term memory at a time. It can be thought of as the mind's white board where the brain works out decisions and problems. Once the board is full, something has to be erased to make more room for the next problem.

The third category is long-term memory, which is essentially the storage center for important information. Aspects of memory can be moved into long-term memory from short-term memory through repetition, meaningful association, powerful emotional connection and so forth. Once information becomes a part of long-term memory, there is typically a very small instance of forgetting it.

This is because long-term memory results from physical changes in the patterns of neurons and synapses in the brain. Long-term memory can be further broken down into several categories. Some memories are explicit and some are implicit.

Implicit memory is an unconscious form of memory, and typically has to do with procedures and patterns of completing a task. Because of this, implicit memory is also known as procedural memory. For example, once a person has learned to tie their shoes or ride a bike, the actions become automatic. They can be performed unconsciously.

In contrast to implicit memories, explicit memories take a conscious effort to be remembered. When a person studies facts for a test or works to memories the names of all the individuals in a class or workplace it is an example of explicit memory. Explicit memory is also known as declarative memory and relates primarily to facts, events, and concepts. It is sometimes further broken down into categories of semantic memory (of facts and concepts) and episodic memory (of events and experiences).

AGORAPHOBIA

Agoraphobia is an anxiety disorder characterized by a fear of public places. Typically, those who experience agoraphobia are plagued by feelings that they will not be able to escape a situation if something goes wrong or if they have a panic attack. Fears of using public transportation, being in open spaces, being in crowded areas, standing in line or leaving their homes are all symptoms of agoraphobia.

For some, their fears prevent them from leaving their homes for long stretches of time. Others require the presence of a trusted friend or relative whenever leaving the home. The National Institute of Mental Health estimated that 5% of individuals develop agoraphobia at some point in their lives, typically in their 20s or 30s.

ETHNOCENTRISM

Ethnocentrism is a perspective of viewing the world through the lens of an individual's own ethnicity or culture. In ethnocentrism, an individual believes that their own culture and belief's are superior to all others, or the "best," or the most natural. While this can be a basis for establishing feelings of patriotism or nationalism, ethnocentrism is generally viewed in a negative context because it supports feelings of disdain, judgment, and discrimination of all who are different.

CULTURAL RELATIVISM

Cultural relativism stands in contrast to ethnocentrism because it takes a much more accepting position. The perspective of cultural relativism is to judge the actions of individuals within the context of their own culture, and that no single culture is superior to another. Different does not equate with worse. Based in this perspective, no culture has the right to impose their views and beliefs on another. It takes into consideration that the different circumstances and beliefs of different cultures lend to different behaviors and outcomes. Because of this, cultural relativism is generally considered a much more acceptable attitude than ethnocentrism.

Geography

Geography is a systematic study of the Earth as the home of human beings. It is from the study of Earth as a huge globe to land forms to water bodies to soil and minerals to climate and how these have a pronounced effect on plant life, animal life or human life.

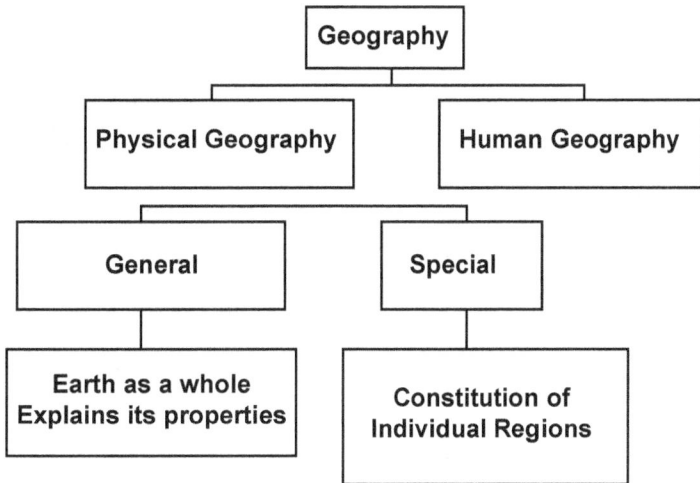

As seen in the chart above, geography deals with physical geography as well as human geography. Then, what is geology? Where does it differ from physical geography? Physical geography deals with the Earth's surface, and is a study of the landscapes and their distinct features, etc.; whereas geology confines itself to the study of how rocks form, their internal structures, how the earth looks inside if you delve deeper and deeper, and how historically the earth has evolved. Geography, in a broader sense, is the study of the Earth by homosapiens.

DISTANCE, ECOLOGY, LOCATION, REGIONAL GEOGRAPHY, SPATIAL INTERACTION, WEATHER AND CLIMATE, ETC.

World Regions are divided into:
- North America
- South America including Latin America and the Caribbean
- Europe
- North, Middle and East Africa
- Sub-Saharan Africa
- Russia – C.I.S. – Central Asia
- South Asia
- East Asia
- South East Asia

- Australia, New Zealand, Pacific (South)

Weather

Different regions of the earth have different weather conditions – temperature, pressure, water and water vapors. Weather is a daily phenomenon affecting the lives of living beings and shaping the landscapes. Weather depends on the movement of air (winds). Weather includes air, rain, clouds, climate (hot, cold), storms, tempests, hurricanes, etc. World regions can also be divided into:

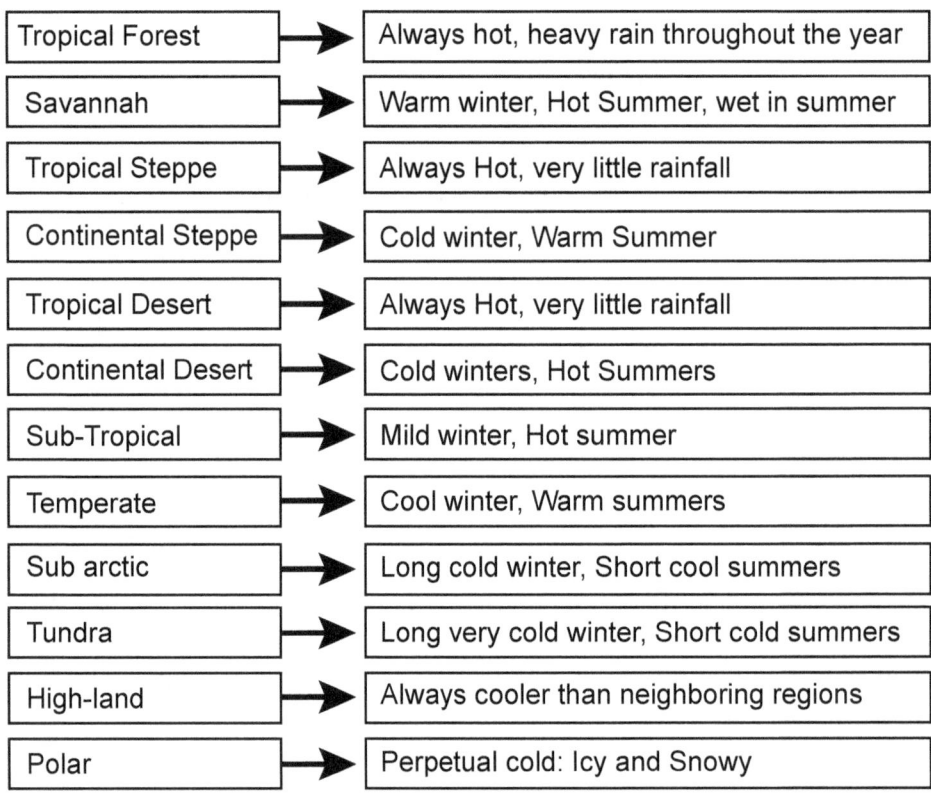

Tropical Forest	Always hot, heavy rain throughout the year
Savannah	Warm winter, Hot Summer, wet in summer
Tropical Steppe	Always Hot, very little rainfall
Continental Steppe	Cold winter, Warm Summer
Tropical Desert	Always Hot, very little rainfall
Continental Desert	Cold winters, Hot Summers
Sub-Tropical	Mild winter, Hot summer
Temperate	Cool winter, Warm summers
Sub arctic	Long cold winter, Short cool summers
Tundra	Long very cold winter, Short cold summers
High-land	Always cooler than neighboring regions
Polar	Perpetual cold: Icy and Snowy

Distance plays an important part in this study. People identify and create regions, and, regions encourage people's activities. When regions are developed through agriculture or industry, lands or industry situated far away from human habitations demand less rent. Locations are known by longitude and latitude, a distance that can isolate locations. Locations can be in different directions; map reading is an integral part of learning geography. Direction is normally shown:

Resource availability, land fertility, technological inputs as well as conducive environment decide the distribution of population. Migratory mobility, Birth and Death rate shape up the demographic component of any given region. When people congregate, language and religion follow. Each region over a period of time develops a distinct culture.

Ecology

It is not only the study of flora and fauna, i.e., plants, animals and their natural surroundings, but also their mutual relationship. "Ecology" is derived from a Greek root "ecos" (literally "oikos") meaning 'house' and "logy" (from "logos") meaning 'study of' or, 'knowledge.' Human beings are the only species that can change the environment itself to suit their way of life.

Spatial Interaction

It may be defined as the contact, movement and linkage between points in space (i.e., between particular locations in different regions). It is concerned with the movement of people, information, capital, goods and traffic between different geographical locations. The spread of people, goods or information across space is referred to as spatial diffusion.

Climate

The climate is the average conditions prevailing in the weather of any given area, measured over a time period (may be many years). Climate changes occur on account of rain, wind, snowfall, temperature, and humidity (the amount of water vapor in the air). Latitude, seashore as well as hilly terrain are a few factors that govern the climate. Life processes depend on climatic factors. When the sun is directly above your head (i.e., 90 degrees), the temperature is the highest. The temperature is the lowest when sunrays move through a thick atmosphere and reach the ground obliquely. This is why there is a temperate zone near the equator; two temperate zones in the mid-latitude as well as the two polar zones. This difference in temperature on Earth sets up a pattern of winds, which has the potential to affect the global climate.

GEOGRAPHY – POINTS TO REMEMBER

- There are 360 degrees of longitude-the circumference of earth – measured in de- grees east or west. Greenwich, England, has 0 degrees longitude.
- There are 180 degrees of Latitude, measured in degrees north or degrees south. At 0 degrees latitude is the Equator.
- GIS – Geographic Information System – Locations, data combined with the application of computers generate GIS, which is used to probe many issues.
- Koppen climate classification system consists of (1) Tropical Moist climates, (2) Dry climates, (3) Moist Mid-Latitude climates with cold winters, (4) Moist Mild-latitude climates with Mild winters, and (5) Polar climates, and is used ex- tensively.

GREAT LAKES

The Great Lakes region of North America is one of the remarkably unique features of the continent. Not only do the five lakes include some of the largest freshwater lakes in the world, they also create a continuous draining canal to the ocean because they are interconnected. The development of these lakes all started around 70,000 years ago with the start of an ice age.

As mile-high walls of ice moved southward, dirt and sediment were picked up and pushed along with it. Not only that, the tremendous weight of the ice compressed the earth below it. When the ice began to recede at the end of the ice age, it revealed gouges in the earth that had been created by the ice. Runoff from the melting glaciers filled the empty space and created what we now know as the Great Lakes. The lightened load on the surface of the earth then allowed the ground to decompress slightly, and created the natural slope in the lakes that formed it as a natural drainage to the ocean.

Introduction to Anthropology

Anthropology may be divided into:

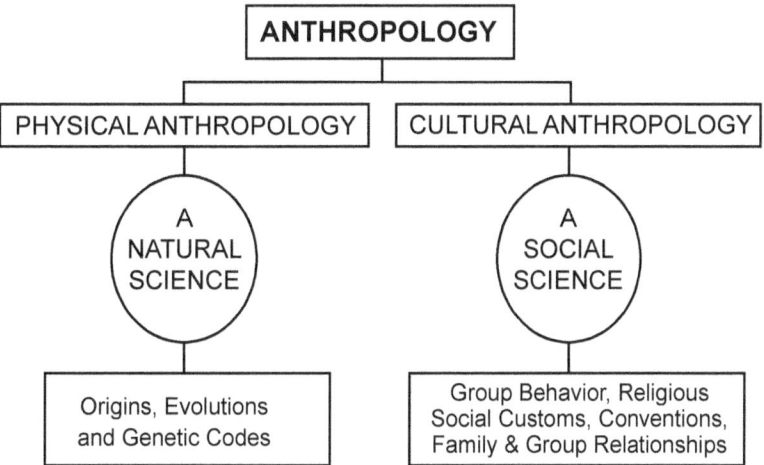

Physical anthropology deals with humans and primates. Physical anthropologists study biological aspects of human beings and primates. They study fossils of once-living humans, and forms similar to humans. They compare and analyze genetic codes and DNA. The word anthropology is derived from the Greek roots "anthropos" – human/man, and "logos," – thought, reason, or study of. The study of human beings, their origin, development, and their culture is what anthropology deals with.

CULTURAL ANTHROPOLOGY

It deals with human behavior in groups, tries to know the origins of religions and how religious beliefs form, seeks to go deep into various customs and conventions and tries to find out family relationships. It tries to explain meaningfully the development of human societies on earth. Difference in terms used:

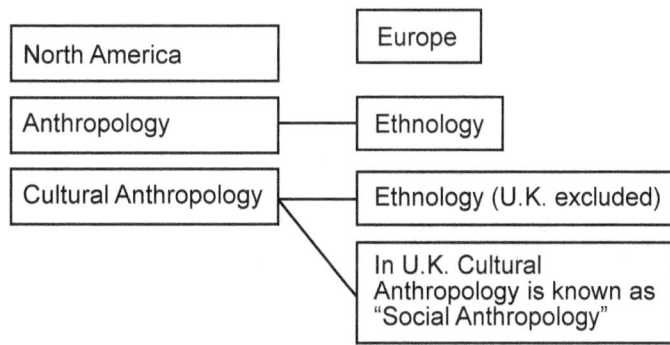

Till the middle of the 20th century, the study of cultural anthropology was confined to primitive cultures, cultures other than Western. However, it now has a very wide scope as the field stretches to include all forms of human association – village societies and communities, urban cultures as well as delving into business and corporate cultures. Social strata and structures, religion, law, art, policies and technologies – all these and more are used to study and comprehend human society as a complex and participative whole (holistic view). Charles Darwin, in 1859, expounded the theory of biological evolution. This lead many anthropologists to study cultural anthropology to arrive at a meaningful discovery. Many views and divergent views came into being.

ETHNOGRAPHY

The basis of ethnography is fieldwork. The anthropologist starts living with people of a given society, whose behavior pattern he is studying. He becomes part and parcel of that society though maintaining a studious non-involvement in the affairs of the society as such. He looks from inside and compiles a descriptive and comprehensive study material for complete analysis.

INTRODUCTION TO ANTHROPOLOGY – POINTS TO REMEMBER

- Primates belong to the class "Mammalia" and order "Theria" which includes spider monkeys, apes, chimpanzees and Homo sapiens (Humans).
- The study of the history as well as the structure of any given language is known as "Linguistics."
- In 1965 Gregor J. Mendel, an Australian monk, compiled the earliest known laws of heredity by studying pea plants.
- Blood Groups O, A, B and AB, were discovered by an Austrian Physician named Karl Land Steiner (Early 20th century).
- According to Lewis H. Morgan of the United States, all societies pass through three distinct stages of evolution, via, savagery, barbarism and finally civilization.
- Herodotus is believed to be the first ethnologist.
- Tacitus, a Roman historian, wrote an anthropological material known as "Germania" in 98 AD that sought to study various Germanic Tribes.

HOMINIDS

Hominids are essentially the precursors to the human race. Several species of hominids have been discovered ranging from those closer to ape-like species to some that were quite similar to humans today. The earliest hominids were found in the grasslands of Africa, primarily in Southern Africa. Over time, hominid civilizations spread throughout Africa and Eastward into Asia. At the time, Europe was covered in ice, but when the ice receded it allowed the spread of hominids to continue throughout the world.

Introduction to Religion

BUDDHISM

Buddhism is a religion based upon the teaching of Buddha, who is said to have spent years in spiritual cultivation to discover the true nature of reality, or enlightenment. Buddhism was mainly concentrated in the Indian sub-continent, but has now increased to worldwide popularity. It is considered a major world religion and has over 350 million followers.

In Buddhism, any person can become enlightened through the study of Buddha's teachings and their practical application. Buddhists are expected to live a life of virtue and morality, and they are to purify their minds. They seek a state of nirvana, or moksha, through the eightfold path and middle way.

JUDAISM

Out of the three largest monotheistic religions in the world, Judaism is the oldest. In fact, it is the parent religion to both Christianity and Islam. Judaism is monotheistic in that it believes in only one true God, who created and continues to rule the world. God is both transcendent and eternal. He is omnipotent. In Judaism, the Jewish people are the "Chosen Ones" in that they are to be an example to all others in the world of God's magnificence.

Jewish religious history is rather extensive, yet there are some major elements that are important to understanding the development of Judaism from its early formation to the religion we know today. Many of the elements are also essential for understanding the foundation of both Christianity and Islam.

Jews have an extensive religious history that can be traced back to the patriarch Abraham. In Abraham's covenant with God, he moved to Canaan around 1800 BC, and God kept his promise to make Abraham the father of a great nation. Through his sons, Isaac and Jacob, Judaism began. While some historians believe that early Jews believed that there were other Gods, but they viewed their God as the sole Creator of everything. Yaweh, or God to the Jews, was a jealous God and required Jews to worship him alone.

By 1600 BC, the Jews migrated to Egypt during a famine. Egypt remained rich with food and water mostly due to the prophecy and dream interpretation of Joseph. After Joseph passed, though, the Pharaoh at the time forgot Egypt's gratitude replacing it with jealousy of the thriving Jews, so he enslaved them. They were held in slavery until 1280 BC when Moses led the people out of Egypt.

While in the desert seeking the land of "milk and honey," otherwise known to Canaan, God gave the Jews the Ten Commandments and many other laws. Through these laws God made a covenant with the Israelites that began the religious tradition inherent in Judaism. Yet it was also during this time that they defied Yahweh, so God made them roam the desert for 40 years prior to letting them enter Canaan around 1200 BC.

Saul then established a kingdom that was then passed on to King David and later Solomon. The capital was in Jerusalem. Yet after the rule of Solomon, the kingdom split in two, establishing the northern kingdom of Israel and the southern kingdom of Judah. In the 8th century BC, Israel was invaded by the Assyrians and conquered. It was not until the 6th century BC that the Babylonian army defeated the kingdom of Judah.

The center of all Jewish worship was the First Temple, and the Babylonians who invaded Judah destroyed it. Meanwhile, the elite of Judah were exiled to Babylonia. During this time the Jews in Babylonia wrote the "Babylonian Talmud" and the Jews that were left in Judea wrote the "Palestinian Talmud," creating the first written form of the Torah and the Talmud used today. Eventually, Persia defeated the Babylonians, and the Jews returned home to build the Second Temple.

ISLAM

Judaism gave birth to two religions. One was Christianity and the other was Islam. Like Christianity and Judaism, Islam is an Abrahamic religion and also monotheistic. The religion is based upon the teachings of Muhammad recorded in the Qur'an, as followers believe in Muhammad as God's final prophet. Believers in Islam are called Muslims.

There are over one billion Muslims, making Islam the second largest religion in the world. Muslims believe that Muhammad received God's final word for humanity and that his teachings will last until the Day of the Resurrection. They believe that the word Muhammad wrote in the Qur'an is flawless and unchangeable and that other religions like Judaism and Christianity have distorted the Word of God in the Hebrew Bible and New Testament. Therefore, the Qur'an is a correction of those errors.

CHRISTIANITY

While Judaism is one of the oldest and largest monotheistic religion, its numbers cannot compare to those of its offshoot, Christianity. In 2001 it was believed that were at least 2.1 billion Christians, which made it the world's largest religion then, and it continues to grow. It is an Abrahamic religion like Judaism and Islam, and much of its foundation can be seen in the Old Testament. It began in the 1st century as a Jewish sect, yet broke off from Judaism to form its own religion.

There are several denominations in Christianity with their own traditions and church bodies. However, whether someone belongs to the branch of Roman Catholicism, Eastern Orthodoxy, or Protestantism, there is a common foundation of beliefs. It is only in the doctrinal differences of custom and place that vary in the branches of Christianity.

Christianity is monotheistic, as they believe that there is one God that created the universe and holds power over it. Where it differs from Judaism is in the idea of the Christ, or Messiah. In early Judaism, messiah was used to name any person appointed as a prophet of God. However, there were numerous Jewish prophecies of a "savior" that would deliver them from their problems with the Romans. The Christian sect, though, believed that this "savior" was to be a spiritual savior.

According to Christian belief, this messiah was associated with numerous prophecies in the Hebrew Bible. He was to be a descendent of David, and would be the new Leader of the Jews. He would rebuild Israel, bring world peace, destroy the evil, and judge the world. Within those prophecies, the Messiah was to be one with God, or he is the God of Abraham, Isaac, and Jacob. He was to die and make atonement for the sins of the people and serve as an example of Godliness to the people.

Christians assert that Jesus of Nazareth fulfilled the prophecies laid out in the Hebrew Bible, or Old Testament, and therefore is the Christ. They believe he will return to fulfill the remainder during the Second Coming. This view is controversial among Jews and Islam, as there were also many warnings of false prophets. However Christians assert that, as Jesus fulfilled all the prophecies of a Messiah, he is the One True Christ.

TAOISM

While Confucianism seeks to perfect people within the world, both in a secular and spiritual way, Taoism is very much its opposite. Taoists prefer to turn away from society, instead becoming fulfilled in a trans-ethical contemplation of nature. One becomes "at one with oneself." There is a quest for freedom from the social constraints present in Confucianism.

Some believe that Taoism is a religion of passive contemplation, but to great Taoist thinker, Lao-tzu and Chuang-tzu encouraged Taoists to transcend the limited existence of the human condition. They wanted to find the mystery of life and steal the secret of Heaven and Earth so that they could become immortal. This striving for immortality is central to Taoism.

The Taijitu is most commonly represented as the Yin and Yang. It is the representation of opposing, and yet complementary, forces in all things.

SHAMANS

In Native American culture spirituality can be very diverse, but most tribes practice a variety of rituals and ceremonies. There is a deep sense of respect for the natural world, and an emphasis on ethics. The most characteristic figures of Native American spirituality are Shamans.

Shamans are believed to be deeply spiritual individuals who have access to the spirit world. Through meditation, chanting, fasting, drumming, and other techniques, Shamans are able to communicate with spirits (both good and bad). The communication can help them to receive information and help in knowing how to heal and help those in the natural world. This is often accomplished while in a trance-like state. Shamans are not limited to healing, however. They are also believed to be able to receive information, including where to hunt, and decisions that should be made.

FIRST GOTHIC CATHEDRAL IN FRANCE

For centuries Roman influences dominated architecture throughout Europe. This began to change in the 1100s when the traditional Romanesque architecture began to be replaced by the Gothic style. Over the next several centuries beautiful Gothic cathedrals that still stand today were built all across Europe. The first such cathedral was the Basilica of St. Denis. The basilica was actually a remodeling of an older church that had stood for hundreds of years.

Abbot Suger was an advisor to the French royalty and convinced them to allow him to rebuild the church to allow for higher traffic of pilgrims coming to pay homage to St. Denis. The benefits of using the gothic style (borrowed largely from Islamic architecture of the time) allowed the creation of the much more open and beautiful space. While the characteristic rounded roman arches of the old style required thick walls and heavy buttressing, the Gothic style featured pointed arches that allowed for narrower support columns and beautiful, large, open windows. This drew attention upwards and therefore towards the heavens. The beauty of the basilica astonished visitors, and it ultimately became the resting place of the French monarchy for several centuries.

Sample Test Questions

An important note about these test questions. Read before you begin. Our sample test questions are NOT designed to test your knowledge to assess if you are ready to take the test. While all questions WILL test your knowledge, many will cover new areas that are not previously covered in this study guide. This is intentional. For questions that you do not answer correctly, take the time to study the question and the answer to prepare yourself for the test.

1) This branch of geography is the science that deals with geographic patterns of species distribution and the processes that result is in patterns. What branch and sub-field of geography does this explain?

   A) Physical Geography – Biogeography
   B) Human Geography – Geosophy
   C) Human Geography – Social Geography
   D) Physical Geography – Geomorphology
   E) Human Geography – Regional Geography

The correct answer is A:) Physical Geography – Biogeography.

2) Who benefited most from the Reconstruction?

   A) Northerners
   B) Southerners
   C) African Americans
   D) European Immigrants
   E) Whites

The correct answer is C:) African Americans. As a part of Reconstruction, each Confederate state had to agree to the 13th, 14th and 15th amendments which ended slavery and gave slaves the right to due process and voting.

3) Which of the following is most likely a primary group?

   A) Quilting clubs
   B) Sports teams
   C) Family
   D) Alcoholics Anonymous
   E) Both A and B

The correct answer is C:) Family. Families interact with each other and care about each other's well being. This makes them primary groups.

4) America declared war on Britain in 1812 due to what event(s)?

   A) Embargo act
   B) The seizure of thousands of American sailors, restraints on neutral trade, and the alliance and military support of Indians blocking American settlement of the Northwest
   C) Treaty of Ghent
   D) Seizure of American sailors, the treaty of Ghent and the embargo act.
   E) Wars between Britain and France, in which both countries had repeatedly violated the rights of Americans

The correct answer is B:) The seizure of thousands of American sailors, restraints on neutral trade, and the alliance and military support of Indians blocking American settlement of the Northwest.

5) Who is credited for the concept of social contracts?

   A) Thomas Malthus
   B) Montesquieu
   C) Plato
   D) Adam Smith
   E) John Locke

The correct answer is E:) John Locke. Locke is also famous for his natural rights philosophy which stated that all men were born with natural rights to life, liberty and property.

6) What was the outcome of the Mexican American War, and the effects it had on the institution of the United States of America?

    A) Upon the beneficial win of the Mexican American War America gained half of the Mexican territory.
    B) The aftermath of the Mexican-American War was favorable to America as it gave them command and the region of Texas joining the American Union.
    C) The Mexican-American War gained the region of California and the respect of the nation.
    D) Upon the beneficial win of the Mexican-American War America gained three-fourths of the Mexican territory.
    E) The aftermath of the Mexican-American War was favorable to the American people who gained the lands of New Mexico, Nevada and California.

The correct answer is A:) Upon the beneficial win of the Mexican American war America gained half of the Mexican territory.

7) Although this war was long and killed thousands of soldiers it brought unity to American society and the most accomplished humanitarian improvement. What war was it and what was the humanitarian improvement that was made?

    A) The War of 1812. Once Britain lost the war they allowed thousands of captured sailors to be releases and they repealed all trade embargoes.
    B) The American Civil War. Southern nationalism was completely abolished allowing unity of the states and all forms of slavery had been completely eliminated.
    C) World War I. The German, Austro-Hungarian, and Russian Empires ceased to exist.
    D) World War II. Britain, France, Germany, and Japan ceased to have great powers in the traditional military sense.
    E) The Mexican-American war. The win over the Mexican-American war offered America more land for westward expansion that included three non-slave holding states.

The correct answer is B:) The American Civil War. Southern nationalism was completely abolished allowing unity of the North and South and all forms of slavery had to be eliminated.

8) Who were most targeted during the Zoot Suit Riots?

    A) Chinese
    B) Whites
    C) Mexican Americans
    D) Japanese
    E) Irish

The correct answer is C:) Mexican Americans. During WWII, riots broke out between Latino youths and military servicemen in the Los Angeles area. These were referred to as the Zoot Suit Riots because of the colorful apparel of the Latino youths. They mainly attacked Mexican-American Marines and Sailors.

9) Which three amendments were implemented with the aftermath of the American Civil war?

    A) The 13th, 14th, and 15th amendments
    B) The 11th, 12th, and 13th amendments
    C) The 14th, 15th, and 16th amendments
    D) The 12th, 13th, and 14th amendments
    E) The 15th, 16th, and 17th amendments

The correct answer is A:) The 13th, 14th and 15th amendments.

10) How many times does the sun pass over the equator in a given year?

    A) 2
    B) 4
    C) 12
    D) 365
    E) None of the above

The correct answer is A:) 2.

Social Sciences & History

11) At the commencement of the American Civil War, seven states seceded. Name those states in order of seceded date.

   A) Georgia, Alabama, Louisiana, Florida, South Carolina, and Texas.
   B) Georgia, Alabama, Louisiana, Florida, Mississippi, Texas, and Virginia.
   C) South Carolina, Mississippi, Florida, Alabama, Texas, Arkansas and Virginia.
   D) South Carolina, Mississippi, Florida, Alabama, Georgia, Louisiana, and Texas.
   E) South Carolina, Mississippi, Florida, Alabama, Georgia, Louisiana, and Arkansas.

The correct answer is D:) South Carolina, Mississippi, Florida, Alabama, Georgia, Louisiana, and Texas.

12) How were the Great Lakes formed?

   A) They were man made
   B) Volcanic activity
   C) Glaciers carved the land and then melted into the water that eventually filled them
   D) An earthquake caused the rivers to flow into the area which eventually filled the lake
   E) The Great Lakes are just a myth

The correct answer is C:) Glaciers carved the land and then melted into the water that eventually filled them. The Lauren-tide glacier covered most of Canada. Its weight carved the Great Lakes and as it melted, the lakes were filled.

13) This method of voting compares every option pair-wise with every other option, one at a time, and an option that defeats every other option is the winner. Which method of voting is described?

   A) Bloc voting
   B) Condorcet voting
   C) Ranked voting
   D) Binary voting
   E) Rated voting

The correct answer is B:) Condorcet voting.

14) Which of the following did President William Taft NOT do after his presidency?

   A) Chancellor Kent Professor of Law and Legal History at Yale Law School
   B) President of the American Bar Association
   C) International Arbitration
   D) Appointed 10th Chief justice
   E) Died of heart disease and blood pressure complications

The correct answer is E:) Died of heart disease and blood pressure complications. Taft did not die of these complications until 1930, 17 years after his presidency.

15) Austria-Hungary, Germany, and the Ottoman Empire were disintegrated due to what major American event?

   A) World War I
   B) The War of 1812
   C) World War II
   D) The War of Independence
   E) The Compromise of 1850

The correct answer is A:) World War I. World War I eventually disintegrated the Empires of the Austria-Hungary, Germany, and Ottoman.

16) When did progressive tax begin?

   A) 1932
   B) 1986
   C) 2001
   D) 1945
   E) 1993

The correct answer is B:) 1986. In 1986 president Regan signed the Tax Reform Act which raised taxes for the upper income Americans and lowered taxes for the lower income Americans.

17) Although many different aspects, combined with time and incidents, caused World War I many individuals had plenty of their own opinions. Who was the President during that time and his opinion of what caused World War I?

   A) President Woodrow Wilson. He and others blamed the war on the assassination of Archduke Franz Ferdinand, the heir to the Austro-Hungarian throne.
   B) President William Howard Taft. He blamed the war on the militarist ideology, which is the doctrinal view of society being best served when people of the militaries concepts govern it.
   C) President William Howard Taft. He and others blamed the war on the assassination of Archduke Franz Ferdinand, the heir to the Austro-Hungarian throne.
   D) President Warren G. Harding. He blamed the war on the militarist ideology, which is the doctrinal view of society being best served when people of the militaries concepts govern it.
   E) President Woodrow Wilson. He blamed the war on the militarist ideology, which is the doctrinal view of society being best served when people of the militaries concepts govern it.

The correct answer is E:) President Woodrow Wilson. He blamed the war on the militarist ideology, which is the doctrinal view of society being best served when people of the militaries concepts govern it.

18) Which of the following was NOT a reason for the Paris Peace Conference?

   A) To deal with the defeat powers of WWI
   B) To set the peace terms for Germany
   C) To reshape the map of Europe
   D) To set the peace terms for Germany's allies
   E) To create the League of Nations

The correct answer is E:) To create the League of Nations. The Paris Peace Conference was not held to create the League of Nations but the League was created during the conference.

19) The panic of 1893 can be greatly contributed to which of the following?

   A) The Sherman Silver Purchase Act
   B) The McKinley Tariff and the Brand-Allison Act
   C) The Bland-Allison act and the Sherman Silver Purchase Act
   D) The Brand-Allison Act
   E) The Sherman Silver Purchase Act and the McKinley Tariff

The correct answer is E:) The Sherman Purchase Act and the McKinley Tariff. The Sherman Purchase Act and the McKinley Tariff largely contributed to the Panic of 1893.

20) Henry David Thoreau was known as

   A) A romantic
   B) A dark romantic
   C) A transcendentalist
   D) A creator of lithographs
   E) None of the above

The correct answer is C:) A transcendentalist.

21) If you were a member of this group in the mid-1900's you would have goals that included preventing war through collective security, attempting to settle disputes between countries by negotiations, and to improve a more global welfare of humanity. Which group would you have been a member of?

   A) The Ku Klux Klan, organized in the 1920's
   B) The League of Nations formed in 1919
   C) The US Securities Commission established in 1934
   D) The National Industrial Recovery Act, founded in 1933
   E) The Federal Emergency Relief Administration, created in 1932

The correct answer is B:) The League of Nations formed in 1919. The League of Nations, which was founded as a result of the Paris Peace Conference in 1919.

22) Federalism is the process by which each citizen is under

   A) The authority of a central national government.
   B) The authority of a regional state government.
   C) The authority of a local city government.
   D) The authority of both a national and state government.
   E) The authority of both a national and city government.

The correct answer is D:) The authority of both a national and state government. The United States operates under a federal system where people are citizens of both the nation (under the Federal Government) and a state (under the individual state governments).

23) How did the role of women change during World War II, also known as the "Rosie the Riveter" phenomenon?

   A) Women were required to join the armed forces as military nurses to aid in the injured soldiers.
   B) Women offered nursing services throughout the duration of World War II.
   C) Women joined the labor workforce in factories and other positions that men normally held.
   D) The majority of women assumed their household positions to keep the soldiers moral and drive up to come home from the war.
   E) Women established military hospitals and homeless shelters for families who lost their fathers and husbands during the war.

The correct answer is C:) Women joined the labor workforce in factories and other positions that men normally held. These jobs included bank tellers, shoe salesmen, and waitress duties.

24) Social psychology, sociology and anthropology have what in common?

   A) They all study how people live and work in groups and communities.
   B) They were all founded by Freud.
   C) They are all in the same college major.
   D) They require accreditation to work in.
   E) None of the above

The correct answer is A:) They all study how people live and work in groups and communities.

25) Established during World War II, what was the responsibility of the Civilian Air Patrol?

   A) Civilians were trained to be air traffic controllers to aid in the tack off and landing of fighter pilots.
   B) Civilians were taught to be lookout on the top of fighter ships that were located on the Pacific Ocean.
   C) Spotters were trained to watch for approaching enemy aircraft in towers along the coastlines and border towns.
   D) Pilots were trained to be wingmen for air pilots, offer support and watch for enemy aircrafts.
   E) A civilian acted as spies in varies locations throughout the world.

The correct answer is C:) Spotters were trained to watch for approaching enemy aircraft in towers along the coastlines and border towns. The Civil Air Patrol is credited with sinking two German U-boats during World War II.

26) Which of the following is NOT true of Roman slaves?

   A) They had no rights
   B) They had legal standing in the court
   C) They could never be free
   D) They were cruel
   E) None of the above

The correct answer is C:) They could never be free. Roman slaves did not have rights, but they could be freed at their master's permission through loyalty or purchasing their freedom. They could also testify at trials.

27) The Civil Rights Act of 1964 was a landmark legislature that was indicted into law on July 2, 1964. What were the major implications of the Civil Rights Act?

A) It protested against the discrimination of individuals based on their race, color, or national origin in voting and employment only.
B) It outlawed discrimination based on race, color, religion, sex, or national origin in voting, employment, and all public services, including transportation and public schooling.
C) It outlawed discrimination based on sex in voting, employment, and public services, including transportation and public schooling.
D) It outlawed discrimination based on race, color, religion, sex, or national origin in voting, employment, and public services, excluding transportation and public schooling.
E) It protested against the discrimination of individuals based on their race, color, sex, or national origin in employment and public services only.

The correct answer is B:) It outlawed discrimination based on race, color, religion, sex, or national origin in voting, employment, and all public services, including transportation and public schooling.

28) Approximately what percentage of Europe was wiped out by the Bubonic plague?

A) 10%
B) 15%
C) 33%
D) 42%
E) 50%

The correct answer is C:) 33%. The Bubonic Plague, or Black Death, was easily spread by rats and fleas along trade routes.

29) If you are a part of a union that "defends and preserves the individual rights and liberties of every person in the United States of America by its own constitution and laws governing it," you are most likely in the…

A) Union Network International
B) American Defense Union
C) American Civil Liberties Union
D) The Universal Defense Union
E) International Union

The correct answer is C:) The American Civil Liberties Union.

30) A group of people with similar backgrounds and culture would be a(n)

   A) Race
   B) Nationality
   C) Ethnicity
   D) Primary group
   E) None of the above

The correct answer is C:) Ethnicity. Ethnicities are based off of cultural similarities, nationalities are based off of citizenship, and race is based off of biological inheritance of traits.

31) President John F Kennedy's stay in office was noted with his famous speech, "Ask not what your country can do for you, but what you can do for your country." How many days, altogether, did President Kennedy serve as the Presi- dent of the United States before his assassination?

   A) 1,000 days
   B) 1,500 days
   C) 900 days
   D) 1,200 days
   E) 950 days

The correct answer is A:) 1,000 days. President John F. Kennedy only served 1,000 days in office before he was assassinated in 1963.

32) Cultural and logistic divisions between East and West Europe initially became divided due to what issue(s)?

   A) Issues of the Alliances and Axes powers of World War II.
   B) Greek speaking eastern lands and the western territories that adopted Latin as their common language.
   C) History of the European empire and the future state of Europe.
   D) Differences in the German reunifications.
   E) Political and economical differences.

The correct answer is B:) Greek speaking eastern lands and the western territories that adopted Latin as their common language.

33) The borders of Western Europe were largely defined by what two major events?

   A) The Civil War and World War I
   B) The Cold War and the Civil War
   C) World War I and World War II
   D) The Civil War and World War II
   E) World War II and the Cold War

The correct answer is E:) World War II and the Cold War.

34) How does a government make up for a budget deficit?

   A) Borrowing more money
   B) Issuing bonds
   C) Lowering taxes
   D) Decreasing the budget for federal aid programs
   E) None of the above

The correct answer is B:) Issuing bonds. Each of the other options either doesn't actually decrease the deficit or makes it worse.

35) A difficult barrier to overcome in middle-eastern culture was the on slot of multiple languages, which were the two widely spoken languages in the Middle East?

   A) Arabic and Persian
   B) Azeri and Greek
   C) Armenian and Greek
   D) Kurdish and Turkish
   E) Hebrew and Turkish

The correct answer is A:) Arabic and Persian. Arabic and Persian were the most widely spoken language in the Middle-East region.

36) During the Greek Dark ages there was very little contact, foreign trade or written or spoken communication coming from Mycenaean civilization in the 11th century BC. Before the Greek Dark ages Mycenaean wrote using Linear B, after the Dark Ages what writing system did Mycenaean use?

A) Lemnos Style
B) Old Italic
C) Syllabary
D) Hellenism
E) Alphabets of Asia Minor

The correct answer is C:) Syllabary.

37) Which of the following is NOT true of the Virginia Resolution at the Constitutional Convention?

A) It proposed that the government be divided into three different branches.
B) It proposed that all representatives be elected by the people.
C) It replaced the Articles of Confederation.
D) It was written by James Madison.
E) It proposed two houses of Congress with representation in one determined by population and the other with equal numbers of representatives from each state.

The correct answer is E:) It proposed two houses of Congress with representation in one determined by population and the other with equal numbers of representatives from each state. The Virginia Plan originally proposed that representation in both houses be determined by population.

38) What is a Japanese shogun?

A) A weapon similar to a sword
B) The chief military commander
C) A soldier
D) A robe only worn on special occasions
E) A tent

The correct answer is B:) The chief military commander.

39) The Roman Empire was the superpower of the known Western World, which was weakened by what conflict?

   A) Between the time of Augustus and the fall of the Western Empire.
   B) The conflict between Gaius Marius and Sulla and the civil war of Julius Caesar against Pompey and Marcus Brutus.
   C) The Battle of Actium.
   D) The Batavian Rebellion.
   E) The Battle of Carrhae.

The correct answer is B:) The conflict between Gaius Marius and Sulla and the civil war of Julius Caesar against Pompey and Marcus Brutus.

40) What is the divine right of kings?

   A) Kings have the right to choose their successor
   B) Kings were given their power by the people
   C) Kings were intended by God to rule from a throne
   D) Kings were intended by God to rule over the people
   E) Kings were intended by God to rule the world

The correct answer is D:) Kings were intended by God to rule over the people.

41) Napoleonic Era, beginning in the early 1800's, began a series of liberal nationalism in Western Europe, which lead to the rise of

   A) The Age of Liberalism
   B) The European Revolution
   C) Democratic systems
   D) The Nazi Party
   E) The Bolshevik Revolution

The correct answer is C:) Democratic systems.

42) Two main concerns over voting rights continue to plague Washington D.C., what are those two voting concerns?

   A) The voting rights of mentally challenged and wounded veterans.
   B) The voting concern over the youngest voters and being uneducated over the issues and the candidates.
   C) The voting rights of the disabled and of those whose primary language is not English.
   D) The voting rights over foreigners and aliens.
   E) The voting rights for senior citizens and those of the volunteers working the voting booths.

The correct answer is C:) The voting rights of the disabled and of those whose primary language is not English.

43) What is ascribed status?

   A) The social status ones parent chooses at birth.
   B) The social status a person takes on voluntarily that reflects both personal ability and merit.
   C) The social status one can achieve.
   D) The social status one is assigned at birth.
   E) The set of rights that comes with ones social status.

The correct answer is D:) The social status one is assigned at birth.

44) The age of _____ was known as the time after World War II when Europe had a strong desire to rebuild and prevent another World War. It was the age when Western Europe and Eastern Europe united under the European Economic Community and signed the Treaty of Rome. This age was known as what?

   A) The age of the Union of Europe
   B) The age of the European Union
   C) The age of the United Europe
   D) The age of European Economics
   E) The age of Europe's Union

The correct answer is B:) The age of the European Union.

45) When were all 50 states ratified?

   A) 1912
   B) 1945
   C) 1920
   D) 1965
   E) 1959

The correct answer is E:) 1959. The 48 states were ratified in 1912 but it wasn't until 1959 that Alaska and Hawaii were ratified as well.

46) Who was the ample mind behind the admission and introduction of the European Union?

   A) Winston Churchill
   B) Robert Shuman
   C) Grand Admiral Karl Donitz
   D) Charles D. Gaulle
   E) King Vittorio Emanuele III

The correct answer is A:) Winston Churchill.

47) The Writ of Habeas Corpus helps uphold which amendment of the constitution?

   A) 4
   B) 5
   C) 12
   D) 15
   E) 18

The correct answer is B:) 5.

48) The Roman Empire contributed a variety of practices and inventions that have served the world and are currently in use today. What are the top three practices that were created or offered by the Roman Empire that are currently in common practice today?

A) Christianity, cement and aspect of modern architecture
B) The calendar, Christianity, and cement
C) The calendar, cement and modern architecture
D) The calendar, Christianity, and aspects of modern architecture
E) Christianity, cement and roads

The correct answer is D:) The calendar, Christianity, and aspects of modern architecture.

49) Which of the following was a political book written in the 1500s?

A) *The Kings Men*
B) *Ode to Joy*
C) *Leaves of Grass*
D) *The Prince*
E) *None of the above*

The correct answer is D:) The Prince. This books was written by Niccolò Machiavelli in 1532. It was political treatise about what Machiavelli thought could unify Italy.

50) Due to the culture of living in tight quarters with domesticated animals and fowl, the epidemics of smallpox, typhus, influenza, diphtheria, and measles killed between 10 to 112 million Indonesians and were introduced to the Americans by which culture?

A) Europeans
B) French
C) Brazilians
D) Indonesians
E) Portuguese

The correct answer is A:) Europeans. The Europeans brought various diseases to America and other countries.

51) Which of the following regulated colonization and trade with Africa?

A) League of Nations
B) Paris Peace Conference
C) Berlin Conference
D) United Nations Conference
E) None of the above

The correct answer is C:) Berlin Conference.

52) The Mediterranean Sea separates Europe from what other continent?

A) Greece
B) Turkey
C) Africa
D) Asia
E) Italy

The correct answer C:) Africa.

53) The beginning of the Westward expansion in 1830 could specifically be attributed to what major event in the US?

A) The American Civil War
B) The Trail of Tears
C) The Treaty of New Echota
D) The Treaty of Ghent
E) The Indian Removal Act

The correct answer is E:) The Indian Removal Act. The Indian Removal Act of 1830 authorized the President to negotiate with Indian tribal lands in the east for lands west of the Mississippi River.

54) What is meant by the phrase "the world is getting smaller"?

   A) The world's circumference shrinks by an average of 1 mile per year.
   B) Modern communication and technology has made travel and intercontinental operations more feasible and common.
   C) As scientists discover more about the universe, the world is viewed as increasingly insignificant.
   D) Technology has reached a high point and cannot advance. Because of this, people's dreams and aspirations are not as high as they used to be.
   E) None of the above

The correct answer is B:) Modern communication and technology has made travel and intercontinental operations more feasible and common. The phrase refers to an increased ability for mobility and long distance communications which creates the perception that the world is smaller.

55) The Congress in Vienna was a conference between major powers of Europe and the Austrian statesman for the purpose of what?

   A) To instill the Christian values of charity and peace from the Europeans to the Australians.
   B) To organize an alliance between the two countries after the defeat of France.
   C) To uphold the settlement following the Napoleonic wars.
   D) To prepare a treaty that would give Europe the power to use Australian lands in exchange for European aid.
   E) To redraw the continents political map after the defeat of Napoleonic France.

The correct answer is E:) To redraw the continents political map after the defeat of Napoleonic France.

56) Who claimed American land for England?

   A) Ferdinand Magellan
   B) John Cabot
   C) Hernando de Soto
   D) Sir John Hawkins
   E) Sir Walter Raleigh

The correct answer is B:) John Cabot. Cabot was originally looking for a passage to India, but instead ended up claiming the eastern coast of North America for England.

57) The period between the death of Alexander the Great and the annexation of the Greek peninsula and the Islands by Rome were considered as what time period?

   A) The late antiquity
   B) Ancient Rome
   C) The fall of Rome
   D) The Hellenistic period
   E) The middle ages

The correct answer is D:) The Hellenistic period.

58) What is a Congressional Committee?

   A) A Congressional subgroup which focuses on a specific issue.
   B) The name used to refer to a meeting of Congress as a whole.
   C) A group of a few people who attempt to sway votes a certain way.
   D) A group which meets to decide nominations for people to run for Congress.
   E) None of the above

The correct answer is A:) A Congressional subgroup which focuses on a specific issue. The range of issues and concerns is so large that without committees it would be nearly impossible to get things done.

59) The term "English Renaissance" refers to, by many historians, a cultural movement in England, between the 1500's and 1600's, that was heavily influenced by, what?

   A) The European Renaissance
   B) The Roman Renaissance
   C) The Italian Renaissance
   D) The French Renaissance
   E) The Greek Renaissance

The correct answer is C:) The Italian Renaissance.

60) What is Gandhi associated with?

   A) Peace
   B) Violence
   C) The United Nations
   D) Hate
   E) Love

The correct answer is A:) Peace.

61) The earliest period in the history of the world, which based on scientific evidence through genetics and the study of fossils places the Homo sapiens in Africa around 200,000 BP is called what?

   A) Paleolithic period
   B) Millennia
   C) Mesolithic period
   D) Pleistocene
   E) Epipaleolithic

The correct answer is A:) Paleolithic period.

62) Which one of the following authors was NOT a transcendentalist?

   A) Ralph Waldo Emerson
   B) Edgar Allen Poe
   C) Henry David Thoreau
   D) Margaret Fuller
   E) Walt Whitman

The correct answer is B:) Edgar Allen Poe.

63) Agriculture has been a major contribution to civilization and mankind, when was the first recording of agriculture, known as the agricultural revolution?

   A) 4000 BC
   B) 2700 BC
   C) 5000 BC
   D) 9500 BC
   E) 6000 BC

The correct answer is D:) 9500 BC.

64) Which of the following believed in a collective unconscious that holds universal human memories?

   A) Alfred Kinsey
   B) Carl Jung
   C) B. F. Skinner
   D) Carl Rogers
   E) Ivan Pavlov

The correct answer is B:) Carl Jung.

65) The first religious beliefs were notably traced to the Neolithic people when it commonly consisted of the worship of the sun and moon. Yet, the earliest sur- viving produced scripture was produced by whom?

   A) The Egyptians
   B) The Kassites
   C) The Inca
   D) The Sumerians
   E) The Azilian

The correct answer is A:) The Egyptians.

66) What two countries repeatedly exploited the people and resources of South America?

   A) Spain and Portugal
   B) Brazil and Spain
   C) Peru and France
   D) Britain and Spain
   E) Portugal and Peru

The correct answer is A:) Spain and Portugal.

67) The "Great Society" goal of eliminating poverty and racial injustice characterized which president?

   A) Richard Nixon
   B) Teddy Roosevelt
   C) Franklin D Roosevelt
   D) Lyndon Johnson
   E) Dwight D Eisenhower

The correct answer is D:) Lyndon Johnson. Much of the legislation passed for the program related to federal aid for the poor.

68) Although the Dutch navigator Willem Janszoon made the first, undisputed, sighting of Australia in 1606, it was not claimed until 1770 by James Cook. What country did he claim the land for?

   A) France
   B) Southeast Asia
   C) Europe
   D) Britain
   E) Rome

The correct answer is D:) Britain.

69) The Trans-Saharan were trade routes where important trades took place between the eighth century and late sixteenth century, using caravans of Arabian Camels through the Sahara desert. With whom did West Africa use the Trans-Saharan to trade?

   A) The Mediterranean countries
   B) The European countries
   C) The Ottoman Empire
   D) The Roman Empire
   E) Spain

The correct answer is A:) The Mediterranean countries.

70) Which of the following is NOT one of the United Nations four main purposes?

    A) To keep peace throughout the world
    B) To develop friendly relations among nations
    C) To stop the production of all weapons of mass destruction
    D) To help nations work together to improve the lives of poor people, conquer hunger, disease, and illiteracy
    E) To be a center for harmonizing the actions of nations

The correct answer is C:) To stop the production of all weapons of mass destruction.

71) Throughout South America, the governments of Argentina, Brazil, Chile and Uruguay were overthrown or displaced by what dictatorship?

    A) The U.S.-aligned military
    B) The Russian military
    C) European military alliance
    D) Chinese military
    E) Britain military

The correct answer is A:) The U.S.-aligned military.

72) What were the black codes?

    A) Unofficial laws enacted right after the civil war that limited the rights and civil liberties of blacks.
    B) official laws enacted right after the civil war that granted rights and liberties to the blacks.
    C) The name by which the Jim Crow laws were known in the south.
    D) Codes enacted after the civil war that made it illegal to discriminate based on ones color.
    E) A set of laws the dictated the labor rate for blacks.

The correct answer is A:) Unofficial laws enacted right after the civil war that limited the rights and civil liberties of blacks.

73) According to Hinduism, which describes a sannayasin?

A) A person who has disavowed any worldly goods in order to life a life of asceticism and seek moksha.
B) The person who uses the Ayurvedic technique to heal illnesses and preserve life.
C) A person who has achieved a oneness of the mind and senses and abandoned all states of existence through Yoga.
D) The person who finds a balance between worldly pleasures and spiritual desires.
E) None of the above

The correct answer is A:) A person who has disavowed any worldly goods in order to life a life of asceticism and seek moksha.

74) This theory of economics relates preferences to consumer demands. What economic theory does this portray?

A) Endogenous growth theory
B) Consumer theory
C) Efficient markets theory
D) Contract theory
E) Production theory basics

The correct answer is B:) Consumer theory.

75) What is psychology?

A) Psychology is the scientific study of the characteristics of mental illness.
B) Psychology is the scientific study of the emotional, social and interpersonal success of humanity.
C) Psychology is the scientific study of the mental process and behavior.
D) Psychology is the scientific study of the evaluation and improvement of mental illness.
E) Psychology is the scientific study of how cognitive and psychological processes affect the human mind.

The correct answer is C:) Psychology is the scientific study of the mental process and behavior.

76) Which of the following is China's main export?

A) Coffee
B) Diamonds
C) Iron and steel
D) Foodstuffs
E) None of the above

The correct answer is C:) Iron and steel.

77) If you belong to a contemporary political party in the United States and your party supports lowered taxes and a limited government in economically chal- lenged areas and your party is more socially conservative and economically libertarian then the others what party do you belong to?

A) Republican Party
B) Democratic Party
C) Farmer-Labor Party
D) Populist Party
E) Socialist Party

The correct answer is A:) Republican Party.

78) With sociology being the study of society and human social interaction, what are the main/basic aspects of sociology, as the nature of sociology?

A) Public sociology, social research, sociological theory, and sociological practice.
B) Social action, social status, social control, and social change.
C) Popular culture, ideology, social research, and sociological theory.
D) Socialization, exploitation, social classes, and sustainable development.
E) Social research, socialization, social change, and social control.

The correct answer is A:) Public sociology, social research, sociological theory, and sociological practice.

79) The Open Door policy related to trade between the United States and

   A) China
   B) Japan
   C) Britain
   D) Australia
   E) Indonesia

The correct answer is A:) China. The purpose of the policy was to allow equal trade opportunities among all countries and China so that one country didn't get a monopoly on trade.

80) Which of the following best describes the beliefs Thomas Malthus?

   A) A good society is one in which the truly wise people are the rulers.
   B) The existence of society is what makes governments necessary, not the other way around.
   C) If the world was run based on capitalist precepts, there would be no need for government.
   D) Eventually the world will run out of resources because population grows exponentially and resources grow geometrically.
   E) None of the above

The correct answer is D:) Eventually the world will run out of resources because population grows exponentially and resources grow geometrically. Malthus believed that limiting factors such as war and disease were nature's way of curbing overpopulation.

81) The third voting rights movement in the 1960's concentrated on advancing the voting age to twenty-one from eighteen, centered on the young boy's who were drafted to fight in a war were ineligible to vote for the leaders who were sending them off to fight. Requiring all states to lower the voting age, which amendment was this?

   A) The twenty-first
   B) The twenty-fifth
   C) The twenty-fourth
   D) The twenty-sixth
   E) The twenty-third

The correct answer is D:) The twenty-sixth. The twenty-sixth amendment advanced the voting age to twenty-one from eighteen.

82) Which of the following is the process of removing an ethnic group from a geographical area by violent and illegal means?

   A) Ethnic cleansing
   B) Civil war
   C) Discrimination
   D) Civil disobedience
   E) None of the above

The correct answer is A:) Ethnic cleansing. Although some of the other terms could apply to a situation in which it happened, A is the most correct answer.

83) What was the freedom bus ride?

   A) A group of people who rode various forms of transportation throughout the northern U.S. to test their rights granted by the Boynton v. Virginia Supreme court decision.
   B) The first group of people to ride a bus from the southern border of the country to the northern border.
   C) A bus that rode right after the civil war informing the country that the blacks were free.
   D) A group of people who rode various forms of transportation throughout the southern U.S. to test their rights granted by the Boynton v. Virginia Supreme court decision.
   E) A free bus that would take voters to the polls.

The correct answer is D:) A group of people who rode various forms of transportation throughout the southern U.S. to test their rights granted by the Boynton v. Virginia Supreme court decision.

84) The original Olympic Games began in what year and in what country?

   A) 776 BC in Athens, Greece
   B) 776 BC in Olympia, Greece
   C) 676 BC in Athens, Greece
   D) 776 BC in Sparta, Greece
   E) 676 BC in Olympia, Greece

The correct answer is B:) 776 BC in Olympia, Greece.

85) The middle ages formed the middle period in a graphic division of European history into three ages. Name those three ages.

   A) The classical civilization of antiquity, the medieval times and the middle ages.
   B) The classical civilization of antiquity, the middle ages and the modern times.
   C) The middle ages, modern times and the renaissance era.
   D) The classical civilization of antiquity, the renaissance era and the modern times.
   E) The medieval times, the middle ages and the modern times.

The correct answer is B:) The classical civilization of antiquity, the middle ages and the modern times.

86) As a definition of American governing ideology, American schools teach three major political inscriptions throughout the school's structures. What are those three inscriptions?

   A) The Constitution, Pledge of Allegiance, and the Bill of Rights.
   B) The Articles of Confederation, the Constitution and the Declaration of Independence.
   C) The Pledge of Allegiance, the Declaration of Independence and the Constitution.
   D) The Constitution, Bill of Rights and the Declaration of Independence.
   E) The Declaration of Independence, the Constitution and the Political Agenda.

The correct answer is D:) The Constitution, Bill of Rights and the Declaration of Independence.

87) The Bay of Pigs

   A) Was successful in overthrowing Cuba
   B) Was successful in overthrowing Japan
   C) Was unsuccessful
   D) Was about farm territory
   E) Was linked to socialism

The correct answer is C:) Was unsuccessful. The Bay of Pigs was an effort to place military trained Cuban exiles back on the island to over throw Castro's regime. The attempt was unsuccessful.

88) After the American Civil war, blacks were given the right to vote, however barriers were implemented including a literacy clause that prevented anyone from voting who could not read or write. A clause was implemented that allowed il- legitimate whites to vote, what was the clause and the format of the clause?

   A) The "Choice of Law" clause allowed any lawmaker or civil service to choose whether to allow the vote of white's who did not pass the literacy test, which they were most likely allowed to vote.
   B) The "Exclusion Clause" exempted the white race from the barriers of the literacy test.
   C) The "Grandfather Clause" waived literacy requirements if one's grandfather was qualified to vote.
   D) The "Privileges Clause" waived the literacy requirements if the individual's family and the individual born within the United States, although if this applied to a person of color they sometimes traced it back three or four generations.
   E) The "Salvatorius Clause" exempted the right for whites from the literacy tests.

The correct answer is C:) The "Grandfather Clause" waived literacy requirements if one's grandfather was qualified to vote.

89) When an adult experiences a trauma and begins to suck their thumb, this is known as

   A) Displacement
   B) Regression
   C) Sublimation
   D) Identification
   E) None of the above

The correct answer is B:) Regression. According to Freud, this is a psychological defense mechanism.

90) Theories of political behavior attempt to explain a person's voting influence and political ideology, with both long-term and short-term voting behaviors. Under these theories what are the short-term factors that effect voting behavior in the United States?

   A) The media and the impact of individual issues.
   B) The campaign debate and campaign commercials.
   C) The individual's teachers, or other educational authority figures and peers.
   D) The individual's family members and the moral goals and family values of the candidate.
   E) The Individuals neighborhood and the candidate's agenda on community improvements.

The correct answer is A:) The media and the impact of individual issues.

91) According to Plato's *Allegory of the Cave*, who should be the rulers in a good society?

   A) The truly wise people
   B) The most experienced people
   C) The wealthiest people
   D) The most intimidating people
   E) None of the above

The correct answer is A:) The truly wise people. The allegory described a group of people who were in a cave and could only see the shadows on the wall of things that passed behind them.

92) International relations theories provide a conceptual model of the analyzing of international relations, with five major theories that are most prevalent. Name those five theories.

   A) Idealism, Marxism, Socialism, Nationalism, and Realism
   B) Realism, Nationalism, Socialism, Functionalism, and Critical Theory
   C) Socialism, Nationalism, Critical Theory, Functionalism, and Anarchism
   D) Socialism, Realism, Communitarianism, Anarchism, and Nationalism
   E) Realism, Idealism, Marxism, Critical Theory, and Functionalism

The correct answer is E:) Realism, Idealism, Marxism, Critical theory, and Functionalism.

93) Copernicus and Galileo relate to what field?

   A) Geology
   B) Biology
   C) Anthropology
   D) Psychology
   E) Astronomy

The correct answer is E:) Astronomy.

94) This theory suggests that the nature of democracy means that democratic countries will not go to war with each other, unless under extreme just cause, but instead have a mutual trust and respect is known as what theory?

   A) The Democratic Peace Theory
   B) The Explanatory Political Theory
   C) The Democracy Peace Theory
   D) The Explanatory Peace Theory
   E) The Democratic Political Theory

The correct answer is A:) The Democratic Peace Theory.

95) The quote "Rather than love, than money, than fame, give me truth," by Henry David Thoreau is characteristic of

   A) Transcendentalism
   B) Utopianism
   C) Deism
   D) Abolitionism
   E) Both A and D

The correct answer is A:) Transcendentalism. The American Transcendentalist movement placed emphasis on life, and transcending from animal or worldly impulses, to more spiritual impulses. Henry Thoreau and Ralph Waldo Emerson are the most famous members of the movement.

96) A foreign policy which combines a non-interventionist military and a political policy of economics nationalism is called what?

A) Leninism
B) Luxemburgism
C) Democratic capitalism
D) Isolationism
E) Internationalism

The correct answer is D:) Isolationism.

97) Which of the following is NOT true of the Renaissance?

A) It centered on a revival of Greek and Roman knowledge.
B) It had a more optimistic view of cities than was held in the Middle Ages.
C) Humanist beliefs flourished during the Renaissance.
D) Art during the Renaissance became more realistic and focused on human beauty.
E) All of the above are true.

The correct answer is E:) All of the above are true. The Renaissance became a rebirth of antiquity in which human knowledge and understanding was viewed more optimistically. The view of cities changed from "full of evil" to places where civic virtue could be practiced.

98) Which of the following best defines cultural relativism?

A) An individual should not be judged based on their culture.
B) An individual's belief and actions should be understood by others of that individual's culture.
C) An individual's belief and actions should be understood by others because of that individual's culture.
D) An individual should decide for themselves their own culture to be a part of.
E) None of the above.

The correct answer is C:) An individual's belief and actions should be understood by others because of that individual's culture.

99) This multi-winner method of voting gives voters fewer votes then the number of seats to be decided. What method of voting is explained?

A) Bloc voting
B) Cumulative voting
C) Rated voting
D) Ranked voting
E) Limited voting

The correct answer is C:) Rated voting. Woman joined the labor workforce in factories and other positions that men normally held, including bank tellers, shoe salesmen, and waitress duties.

100) Which of the following individuals was a strong advocate in encouraging many of Franklin D Roosevelt's New Deal programs?

A) Phyllis Schlafly
B) C. Wright Mills
C) Voltaire
D) Frances Perkins
E) None of the above

The correct answer is D:) Frances Perkins. Perkins was dedicated to social reform throughout her life. When Roosevelt was elected president in 1932, he appointed Perkins as his Secretary of Labor. Throughout his presidency Perkins was a critical supporter of "New Deal" programs that would bring reform to the workplace. She was instrumental in the development of Social Security and the Fair Labor Standards Act.

101) In this Sociology theory it is believed that social process should be studied in terms of cause and effect using the scientific method. Name this theory.

A) Social Positivism
B) Social Constructionism
C) Interpretative Sociology
D) Social System Paradigm
E) Conflict Theory

The correct answer is A:) Social Positivism.

102) In 1838-1839, Cherokee Indians faced hunger, disease and death due to which event?

A) Smallpox
B) King Philip's War
C) Trail of Tears
D) The Seminole War
E) The Sand Creek Massacre

The correct answer is C:) Trail of Tears. Over a quarter of the Cherokee Nation died during the forced migration from Mississippi to Oklahoma.

103) What is the basic concept of the sociology theory of Social Contructionism?

A) A sociological theory is an attempt to reconcile the theoretical split of social systems such as agency/structure, subjective/objective, and micro/macro perspectives.
B) A sociological theory that sees society as made up of inter-dependent sections that work together to fulfill the functions necessary for the survival of society as a whole.
C) A sociological study on dialectical idealism that focuses on the non-physical and psychological revolution.
D) A sociological theory of knowledge that considers how social phenomena develops in distinct social contexts.
E) A sociological theory that attempts to explain social institutions as a means to fill biological needs.

The correct answer is D:) A sociological theory of knowledge that considers how social phenomena develops in distinct social contexts.

104) If you are studying Ethnomethodology what will your focus of study be on?

A) The social connection and interactions of individuals in a virtual setting, such as chat rooms and online message boards.
B) The ways people make sense of their world, display their understanding to others and the shared order in which people live.
C) The study of conflict between social classes and the opposing ideology of those classes.
D) The aspects of social interactions within group settings and the dynamics of individuals' perception of self.
E) The ways environment and the media effect social change and alienation.

The correct answer is B:) The ways people make sense of their world, display their understanding to others and the shared order in which people live.

105) Which of the following is a depressant and is linked to depression?

   A) PCP
   B) Alcohol
   C) Sugar
   D) Saccharine
   E) None of the above

The correct answer is B:) Alcohol.

106) The three main modern sociological theories include:

   A) Systems theory, Postmodernism, and Conflict Theory.
   B) Functionalism, Structural Functionalism, and Symbolic Interactionism.
   C) Postmodernism, Systems Theory and Conflict Theory.
   D) Marxism, Phenomenology, and Symbolic Interactionism.
   E) Conflict Theory, Structural Functionalism, and Symbolic Interactionism.

The correct answer is E:) Conflict theory, Structural Functionalism, and Symbolic Interactionism.

107) During what time period were the Marlboro Man and M&M's created?

   A) 1940 - 1955
   B) 1980 - 1995
   C) 2000 - 2003
   D) 1600 - 1615
   E) 1910 - 1924

The correct answer is A:) 1940 - 1955. The Marlboro Man was first conceived in 1954 and M&M's were invented in 1941.

108) Which three other fields of social sciences have greatly influenced and shared in a great amount of history and common research interest with sociology?

   A) Political Science, Linguistics, and Anthropology
   B) Psychology, Anthropology, and Economics
   C) Linguistics, Economics, and Psychology
   D) Geography, Political Science, and Economics
   E) Psychology, Political Science, and Anthropology

The correct answer is B:) Psychology, Anthropology, and Economics.

109) Which Sociology method are you using if the information you are obtaining takes an extended period of time, ranging from a few months to years, to collect and you monitor a specific group of people?

   A) Case studies
   B) Historical research
   C) Participant observation
   D) Interviewing
   E) Survey research

The correct answer is C:) Participant observation.

110) This sub-field of physical geography is the study of landforms, including their origin and the evolution process, and the processes that shape them. Which sub-field of physical geography is depicted?

   A) Geomorphology
   B) Biogeography
   C) Geodesy
   D) Pedology
   E) Glaciology

The correct answer is A:) Geomorphology.

111) How has the Internet affected the research and study of sociology?

   A) It has offered a new form of research, communication and tools for the study of sociology.
   B) The internet has made available more powerful research tools and visual aids in the concept of understanding sociology better.
   C) The internet has allowed sociologists to compare with other sociologists studies and theories for further accuracy of sociology.
   D) It has given sociologists a variety of aspects for the continued study of sociology through a variety of mediums.
   E) It has given sociologist a broader and more comprehensive research tool and a productive way of using discussion platforms, by using online questionnaires as apposed to paper questionnaires.

The correct answer is E:) It has given sociologist a broader and more comprehensive research tool and a productive way of using discussion platforms, by using online questionnaires as apposed to paper questionnaires.

112) The study of how social behavior and organization has been influenced by evolution and other biological processes is?

   A) Applied sociology
   B) Sociobiology
   C) Sociolinguistics
   D) Social psychology
   E) Comparative sociology

The correct answer is B:) Sociobiology.

113) The study of both healthy individuals and patients who have suffered from a brain injury or a mental illness is what method of psychological research?

   A) Longitudinal studies
   B) Neuropsychological method
   C) Computational modeling
   D) Action research
   E) Controlled experiments

The correct answer is B:) Neuropsychological method.

114) Psychology describes and attempts to explain consciousness, behavior and what?

   A) Social interaction
   B) The nervous system
   C) The mental process
   D) The brain
   E) Relationships

The correct answer is A:) Social interaction.

115) If you study the nature of psychopathology and its causes, having this knowledge applied to clinical psychology for treating patients with psychological disorders you are studying what?

   A) Personality psychology
   B) Social psychology
   C) Abnormal psychology
   D) Cognitive psychology
   E) Comparative psychology

The correct answer is C:) Abnormal psychology.

116) What is the interface between psychology and forensic psychology?

   A) All psychological services in the study of physical stimulation is forensic psychology, senses is the interface.
   B) All psychological services in the occupational fields are forensic psychology, workplace issues is the interface.
   C) All psychological services in experimental manipulation is forensic psychology, evidence based practice is the interface.
   D) All psychological services in perceptions and feelings are forensic psychology, emotions are the interface.
   E) All psychological services performed for the legal community is forensic psychology, the law is the interface.

The correct answer is E:) All psychological services performed for the legal community is forensic psychology, the law is the interface.

117) This field of research psychology involves the application of statistical analysis to psychological research and the development of statistical approaches for measuring and explaining human behavior. What form of research psychology is explained?

   A) Social psychology
   B) Quantitative psychology
   C) Comparative psychology
   D) Cognitive psychology
   E) Developmental psychology

The correct answer is B:) Quantitative psychology.

118) What is the difference between applied psychology and research psychology?

   A) Applied psychology studies the behavior of the mentally ill, while research psychology studies the behavior of individuals who have psychological problems.
   B) Applied psychology uses more controlled experiments of research while research psychology uses the neuropsychological methods.
   C) In applied psychology research is used in an applied setting, while in research psychology the research is only used in an academic setting.
   D) Applied psychology is more driven towards the actions of patients, while research psychology is more driven toward the emotions of patients.
   E) Applied psychology is motivated by the personal change for the future of patients, while research psychology is motivated by the personal change from the past.

The correct answer is C:) In applied psychology the research is used in an applied setting, while in research psychology it is only used in an academic setting.

119) The Berlin Conference of 1884 was called for the purpose of

   A) Establishing boundaries between Middle Eastern nations
   B) Partitioning the remaining unclaimed lands of Africa
   C) Ending the conflicts of WWI
   D) Establishing fair trade practices between European nations and China
   E) None of the above

The correct answer is B:) Partitioning the remaining unclaimed lands of Africa. As rivalries between nations began to get heated, a conference was called by German Chancellor Otto von Bismarck for the purpose of partition the remaining unclaimed lands of Africa. The partitions were based on an agreement to spread Christianity, increase trade, and establish a physical presence in the regions.

120) This research method has merged in recent years to become a significant method of intervention, development and change within groups and communities. What research method is described?

   A) Experimental study
   B) Correlational research
   C) Cross-sectional study
   D) Participatory action research.
   E) Longitudinal study

The correct answer is D:) Participatory action research.

121) This form of psychology examines the internal mental processes such as problem solving, memory, and language. What form of psychology does this depict?

A) Developmental psychology
B) Cognitive psychology
C) Social psychology
D) Emotion psychology
E) Personality psychology

The correct answer is B:) Cognitive psychology.

122) Structuration theory identifies three types of structures in social systems: Signification, which produces meaning through organized language, Legitimation, which produces a moral order through naturalization in societal norms, values and standards and what? Please name and explain the third type of structure.

A) Justification, which produces the order of judgment in a societal fashion.
B) Ramification, which produces the order of social practice through space and time.
C) Domination, which produces power that originates through the control of resources.
D) Socialization, which produces a sequence of proportioned social interactions.
E) Determination, which produces the power struggle of individual purpose.

The correct answer is C:) Domination, which produces power that originates through the control of resources.

123) Specialized techniques are used in the field of economics; they include mathematical economics, econometrics, and computational economics. What is one other important technique used, which summarizes economic activity?

A) Agent-based computational economics
B) Microeconomics
C) National accounting
D) Computer calculations
E) Neoclassical economics

The correct answer is C:) National accounting.

124) What is the study of economics?

A) The study of the investment market and how that affects the economy of the country.
B) The study of capitalism.
C) The study on how to satisfy unlimited wants with limited resources.
D) The study on the financial structure of businesses and the nation.
E) The study of production, distribution and consumption of goods and services.

The correct answer is E:) The study of production, distribution and consumption of goods and services.

125) A branch of economics that studies how individuals, households and firms make decisions to allocate limited resources, normally in a market where goods and services are being bought and sold, is called what?

A) Microeconomics
B) Positive economics
C) Mainstream economics
D) Macroeconomics
E) Normative economics

The correct answer is A:) Microeconomics.

126) The three main concerns of political philosophy include; the political economy by which property rights are defined and access to capital is regulated, the demands of justice in distribution and punishment, and what other concern?

A) Cultural and gender debates as it relates to politics.
B) The rights and freedoms by which it should protect.
C) The various forms of political behavior and political organizations.
D) The theology of the government and political views.
E) The rules of truth and evidence that determine judgments in the law.

The correct answer is E:) The rules of truth and evidence that determine judgments in the law.

127) Recently economic theory has moved toward the study of economic fluctuation rather than _____, yet some economists continue to use the phrase for convenient shorthand. What phrase is this referring to?

   A) Commodity markets
   B) Event study
   C) Business cycle
   D) Economic policy
   E) Production theory basics

The correct answer is C:) Business cycle.

128) What is the name for the Jewish Holiday which is celebrated as the Day of Atonement?

   A) Yom Kippur
   B) Lag BaOmer
   C) Tzom Gedalia
   D) Rosh Hashanah
   E) None of the above

The correct answer is A:) Yom Kippur.

129) This term is used to describe, in fiscal value, the total yearly flow of goods and services in the economy of the nation. What is the term?

   A) Environmental finance
   B) Investment-specific technological progress
   C) Gross National Product
   D) Homogeneous products
   E) Evolutionary economics

The correct answer is C:) Gross National Product.

130) Which branch of economics attempts to answer the following questions: How the prices of financial assets are determined, the effects of a company's methods of financing its operations, and what portfolio of assets should an investor have to meet his objectives?

A) Public finance
B) Industrial organization
C) Institutional economics
D) Financial economics
E) Development economics

The correct answer is D:) Financial economics.

131) The branch of economics that incorporates valued judgments about what the economy should be like or what particular policy action should be recom- mended to achieve a desirable goal is what?

A) Mainstream economics
B) Normative economics
C) Positive economics
D) Heterodox economics
E) Microeconomics

The correct answer is B:) Normative economics.

132) What is the focus of positive economics and how does it differ from other branches of economics?

   A) It focuses on the people, institutions, and their relationships to resources. Positive economics describes the affects of money and supply growth whereas others also instruct on what policy should be followed.
   B) It focuses on how individuals, households and firms make decisions regarding limited resources. Positive economics describes the affects of money and supply growth whereas others also instruct on what policy should be followed.
   C) It focuses on the methods of promoting economical growth. Positive economics describes money and supply affect the nation whereas others also instruct on what policy should be followed.
   D) It focuses on the performance, structure and behavior of the economy as a whole. Positive economics describes what policy should be implemented whereas others describe the affects of certain policies.
   E) It focuses on the cause and effect of relationships and the testing of economic theories. Positive economics describes the affects of money and supply growth whereas others also instruct on what policy should be followed.

The correct answer is E:) It focuses on the cause and effect of relationships and the testing of economic theories. Positive economics describes the affects of money and supply growth whereas others instruct on what policy should be followed.

133) The Keynesian economic perspective advocates which of the following to cure a struggling economy?

   A) Wait and the problem will work itself out eventually
   B) Elect an entirely new set of government officials
   C) Increase the amount of government spending
   D) Decrease taxes
   E) Both C and D

The correct answer is E:) Both C and D. The intended effect is to offset the decrease in spending by businesses and consumers. This should ultimately level out GDP and increase employment. With time the process should be reversed to repay any debts incurred by the government.

134) Unrestricted submarine warfare by Germany is what spurred US engagement in which war?

A) War of 1812
B) Spanish-American War
C) German Conflict of 1898
D) WWI
E) WWII

The correct answer is D:) WWI. Although the United States had sought to maintain neutrality, American deaths that resulted from Germany submarine warfare pushed President Wilson to begin preparations for war. When the Zimmerman Telegram confirmed German intentions to pull the U.S. into the war, Congress agreed to a declaration of war in 1917.

135) The first Gothic Cathedral in France was

A) Notre Dame Cathedral
B) Basilica of St. Denis
C) Salisbury Cathedral
D) Lyon Cathedral
E) Church of Saint-Maclou

The correct answer is B:) Basilica of St. Denis. Abbot Suger was an advisor to the French royalty and convinced them to allow him to rebuild the church to allow for higher traffic of pilgrims coming to pay homage to St. Denis. The church ultimately became the burial place of French royalty for several hundred years.

136) The method of political science used for obtaining evidence of casual effects by evaluating the varying forms of government in the world, and the states they govern, would be considered?

A) International relations
B) Foreign policy analysis
C) Comparative government
D) Comparative environments
E) Foreign policy doctrine

The correct answer is C:) Comparative government.

137) Explain the study and process of human geography.

   A) This branch of geography describes the various aspects of interactions between humans and the natural world.
   B) This branch of geography studies the areas of high populations with a concentration of infrastructures and the interactions of human behavior.
   C) This branch of geography focuses on the study of patterns and processes that shape human interaction with various environments.
   D) This branch of geography studies the impact of security and the prosperity of the nations and human behavior to each.
   E) This branch of geography studies Earth's geography and its relationship with economic development.

The correct answer is C:) This branch of geography focuses on the study of patterns and processes that shape human interaction with various environments.

138) Voltaire was one of the great minds of which historic period?

   A) Enlightenment
   B) Renaissance
   C) Dark Ages
   D) Classical
   E) Neoclassical

The correct answer is A:) Enlightenment. Born Francois-Marie Arouet, Voltaire was a sharp critic of Catholic dogmas and French institutions that prohibited progression. He was a strong advocate of Enlightenment ideals. Although he was imprisoned several times throughout his life, he continued to write countless articles, plays, and scientific works.

139) In this method of geography it deals with quantitative data analysis specifically the application of statistical methodology to the exploration of geographic phenomena. Which method of geography would this be considered?

   A) Epidemiology
   B) Remote sensing
   C) Ethnographical
   D) Geographic qualitative method
   E) Geostatistics

The correct answer is E:) Geostatistics.

140) Geographers use four interrelated approaches to geographical techniques. Name those four approaches.

A) Systematic, geostatistics, regional and descriptive
B) Systematic, ethnography, geostatistics and cartography
C) Systematic, regional, descriptive and analytical
D) Systematic, cartography, descriptive and analytical
E) Systematic, remotes sensing, cartography and analytical

The correct answer is C:) Systematic, regional, descriptive and analytical.

141) The two major fields that economics are divided into are?

A) Neoclassical economics and experimental economics
B) Institutional economics and international economics
C) Labor economics and public finance
D) Economic geography and economics of security
E) Microeconomics and macroeconomics

The correct answer is E:) Microeconomics and macroeconomics.

142) Explain the study of palaeogeography, often called paleogeography, and the branch of geography that it stems from.

A) Palaeogeography is the study of the region and of all its shape and sizes across the earth. It is a sub-field of human geography.
B) Palaeogeography is the study of inland waters including their biology, physical geological, chemical and hydrological aspects. It is a sub-field of physical geography.
C) Palaeogeography is the study of the measurement and representation of the Earth, its gravitational field and other geodynamic phenomena. It is a sub-field physical geography.
D) Palaeogeography is the study of ancient geological environments of the Earths surface. It is a sub-field of physical geography.
E) None of the above

The correct answer is D:) Palaeogeography is the study of ancient geological environments of the Earths surface. It is a sub-field of physical geography.

143) The study of marking maps is known as

   A) Cartography
   B) Geography
   C) Strategic geography
   D) Anthropology
   E) Thermography

The correct answer is A:) Cartography.

144) The primary way in which governments fund deficit spending is

   A) Corporate securities
   B) Tax credits
   C) Printing money
   D) Bonds
   E) None of the above

The correct answer is D:) Bonds. A bond is essentially a short term loan where the issuer (the government) promises to pay back a certain amount at a certain time in the future. Theoretically, bonds are issued in a period of deficit, and paid back in a time of surplus.

145) Phyllis Schlafly is known for her opposition to the

   A) Platt Amendment
   B) Gulf of Tonkin Resolution
   C) Equal Rights Amendment
   D) Civil Rights Act
   E) Teller Amendment

The correct answer is C:) Equal Rights Amendment. Phyllis organized rallies, baked bread for legislators, and appeared on television all in an effort to prevent the passage of the amendment. She argued that the amendment would destroy conservative family values, and strongly disadvantage full time homemakers. Due in large part to her efforts, the amendment was never passed.

146) This branch of geography focuses on geography as an earth science. It attempts to understand the features of the Earth and its environment. Which branch of geography does this represent?

   A) Environmental geography
   B) Earth science
   C) Human geography
   D) Geomatics
   E) Physical geography

The correct answer is E:) Physical geography.

147) This field of anthropology studies the contemporary distribution and the form of artifacts, with the intention of understanding ancient populations, development of human social organization and relationships in population. What form of Anthropology does this describe?

   A) Forensic anthropology
   B) Archaeology
   C) Medical anthropology
   D) Primatology
   E) Human and population genetics

The correct answer is B:) Archaeology.

148) This very significant and famous anthropologist played a key role in organizing the American Anthropological Association, wrote an important book, *The Mind of Primitive Man*, which would dominate American anthropology for the fifteen years, and also brought noteworthy change and theories to cultural anthropology, linguistics, and physical anthropology. Who is this significant figure in anthropology?

   A) Bronislaw Malinowski
   B) E.B. Tylor
   C) George Mercer Dawson
   D) Franz Boas
   E) Margaret Mead

The correct answer is D:) Franz Boas.

149) This study of the Earth's geography and its relationships with economic development is closely related to economic geography and development economics. Which sub-field of geography does this depict?

A) Development geography
B) Political geography
C) Strategic geography
D) Social geography
E) Cultural geography

The correct answer is A:) Development geography.

150) This field of anthropology is the investigation of the culture and social organizations of a particular cultural group. Which field of anthropology does this explain?

A) Socio-cultural anthropology
B) Ethnic anthropology
C) Anthropology of religion
D) Psychological anthropology
E) Social anthropology

The correct answer is A:) Socio-cultural anthropology.

151) The first hominids lived in the grasslands of which continent?

A) North America
B) Asia
C) Australia
D) Europe
E) Africa

The correct answer is E:) Africa. The earliest hominids were found in the grasslands of Africa, primarily in Southern Africa. Over time hominid civilizations spread throughout Africa and Eastward into Asia. At the time Europe was covered in ice, but when the ice receded it allowed the spread of hominids to continue throughout the world.

152) What was Paul of Tarsus' originally intending to do when he reached Da- mascus?

   A) Worship at the Temple
   B) Arrest members of the Christ-worshipping church
   C) Convert people to Christianity
   D) Receive communion
   E) None of the above

The correct answer is B:) Arrest members of the Christ-worshipping church.

153) Which value is not Taoist?

   A) Formal education
   B) Simplicity
   C) Spontaneity
   D) Appreciation of nature's movements
   E) None of the above

The correct answer is A:) Formal education.

154) During which holiday does Islam require fasting?

   A) Al-Hijira
   B) Ramadan
   C) Hajj
   D) Aid al-Haddah
   E) None of the above

The correct answer is B:) Ramadan.

155) Approximately how many Jews are in Spain today?

   A) 100
   B) 1,200
   C) 12,000
   D) 150,000
   E) None of the above

The correct answer is C:) 12,000.

156) Which of these groups was the most liberal thinking in Ancient China?

   A) Xunzi
   B) Taoists
   C) Reformers
   D) Confucians
   E) None of the above

The correct answer is B:) Taoists. Taoism and Buddhism are the two most common religions in China.

157) Christians use this term that refers to the Second coming of Jesus Christ

   A) Messiah
   B) Revelation
   C) Rapture
   D) Liturgy
   E) None of the above

The correct answer is C:) Rapture.

158) Ralph Waldo Emerson was known as

   A) A romantic
   B) A dark romantic
   C) A transcendentalist
   D) A creator of lithographs
   E) None of the above

The correct answer is C:) A transcendentalist.

159) Jews traditionally hang this item in a doorway which contains a scroll of parchment containing the opening lines of the shema in order to remember their religious obligation to God.

   A) Tephllin
   B) Tallit
   C) Kippah
   D) Mezuzah
   E) None of the above

The correct answer is D:) Mezuzah.

160) Each field of anthropology draws from a variety of sub-fields for research, study and methods, which related fields does linguistics anthropology, which seeks to understand the process of human communication, draw from?

A) Ethnic studies, cultural studies, anthropology of media, historical linguistics, and discourse analysis.
B) Cultural studies, anthropology of media, cognitive linguistics, sociolinguistics and narrative linguistics.
C) Sociolinguistics, cognitive linguistics, semiotics, discourse analysis, and narrative analysis.
D) Cultural anthropology, social anthropology, cognitive linguistics, narrative linguistics and sociolinguistics.
E) Narrative linguistics, sociolinguistics, historical linguistics, cognitive linguistics, and narrative analysis.

The correct answer is C:) Sociolinguistics, cognitive linguistics, semiotics, discourse analysis, and narrative analysis.

161) Which religion believes that there is only one God and Mohammad is his prophet?

A) Islam
B) Christianity
C) Judaism
D) Hinduism
E) Taoism

The correct answer is A:) Islam.

162) The ability of an individual to tie their shoes with little conscious thought is a result of which type of memory?

A) Procedural memory
B) Explicit memory
C) Sensory memory
D) Long-term memory
E) Episodic memory

The correct answer is A:) Procedural memory. Procedural memory is also known as implicit memory. These are memories that are specifically related to performing certain actions (or procedures) that become almost automatic due to frequent repetition. Over time these actions essentially become automatic because they have been stored in this portion of long-term memory.

163) Which of the following is NOT a category of long-term memory?

A) Procedural memory
B) Declarative memory
C) Implicit memory
D) Sensory memory
E) Explicit memory

The correct answer is D:) Sensory memory. Sensory memory has the shortest span, typically less than one second, and processes the greatest amount of information. It holds the record of all events relating to the five senses. If information isn't immediately important, it is typically forgotten instantly.

164) If an individual faces extreme anxiety over leaving their home, they may have

A) Agliophobia
B) Arachnophobia
C) Agoraphobia
D) Claustrophobia
E) Mysophobia

The correct answer is C:) Agoraphobia. Agoraphobia is an anxiety disorder characterized by a fear of public places. Fears of using public transportation, being in open spaces, being in crowded areas, standing in line or leaving their homes are all symptoms of agoraphobia.

165) Which of the following terms BEST describes Kurdistan?

A) State
B) Nation-state
C) Cultural anomaly
D) City-state
E) Stateless nation

The correct answer is E:) Stateless nation. Although Kurdistan existed as an independent nation from 1920-1923, it has not existed as an independent state since then, and as a result is considered to be the world's largest stateless nation. Although the Kurdish people possess a distinct culture, language, centralized location and ethnicity, they are citizens over several nations without their own globally recognized government.

166) The case of McCulloch v. Maryland established the right of Congress to

A) Impose a draft
B) Charter a bank
C) Tax state banks
D) Establish school systems
E) None of the above

The correct answer is B:) Charter a bank. In this case, the Supreme Court ruled that Congress did have the right to establish a bank, and that the state of Maryland could not interfere by taxing that bank. It expanded the right of Congress beyond those specifically established in the constitution, and reaffirmed that Congress could take any "necessary and proper" actions in the course of completing its duties.

167) If a person has the opinion that "all foreign food is gross," they could be described as having which perspective?

A) Biodidactic
B) Cultural relativist
C) Egotistical
D) Racist
E) Ethnocentric

The correct answer is E:) Ethnocentric. Ethnocentrism is a perspective of viewing the world through the lens of an individual's own ethnicity or culture. In ethnocentrism, an individual believes that their own culture and beliefs are superior to all others.

168) Which of the following BEST describes cultural relativism?

A) All cultures are related because they derive from a single source.
B) Cultures should be judged relative to the culture an individual is a part of.
C) Actions of individuals should be judged within the context of their own culture, and no single culture is superior to another.
D) Everyone should strive to like other cultures better than their own.
E) Both A and B

The correct answer is C:) Actions of individuals should be judged within the context of their own culture, and no single culture is superior to another. The perspective of cultural relativism stands in contrast to ethnocentrism where one's culture is considered superior to all others. In cultural relativism, different does not equate with worse.

169) The theory of Sociological Imagination is a product of

   A) John Maynard Keynes
   B) William Marbury
   C) Phyllis Schafly
   D) C. Wright Mills
   E) John Adams

The correct answer is D:) C. Wright Mills. C. Wright Mills (1916-1962) was an influential sociologist in the early 1900's. He is most well known for two of his books: *The Power Elite* (1956) and *The Sociological Imagination* (1959).

170) The case of Marbury v. Madison established

   A) The right of Congress to establish a national bank
   B) Congressional powers to overrule the Supreme Court
   C) The Presidential power of veto
   D) The right of the court to issue a writ of mandamus
   E) The Supreme Court's power of judicial review

The correct answer is E:) The Supreme Court's power of judicial review. This was the first case in which the Supreme Court stated their right to declare an act of the legislature to be unconstitutional, and it established the power of judicial review that is still in effect today.

171) The Great Lakes were developed as a result of

   A) Volcanic activity
   B) Vigorous effort by early American colonists
   C) Glacial expansion and contraction
   D) Prehistoric earthquakes
   E) None of the above

The correct answer is C:) Glacial expansion and contraction. Around 70,000 years ago, at the start of the ice age, mile-high walls of ice began to cover the area. When the ice began to recede at the end of the ice age, it revealed gouges in the earth that had been created by the ice. Runoff from the melting glaciers filled the empty space and created what we now know as the Great Lakes.

172) The United States purchased Alaska from which country?

   A) Great Britain
   B) Russia
   C) France
   D) Spain
   E) Canada

The correct answer is B:) Russia. When wars forced Russia to search for funds, they offered sale of Alaska to the United States. Although the purchased was originally considered a great mistake, the discovery of gold mines made Alaska a very important asset to the growing nation.

173) Which man centered his presidency on the campaign of creating a "Great Society"?

   A) Lyndon B Johnson
   B) John F Kennedy
   C) Rutherford B Hayes
   D) Theodore Roosevelt
   E) None of the above

The correct answer is A:) Lyndon B Johnson. Johnson's challenge to the American people was to build a "great society" and seek to cure many of the traditional ills of poverty and misfortune. He won the election with the greatest popular margin in history - 15 million votes.

174) Which of the following was NOT addressed as part of the "Great Society" movement in the 1960's?

   A) Poverty
   B) Civil rights
   C) Education
   D) Medicare
   E) All of the above were passed as part of the "Great Society"

The correct answer is E:) All of the above were passed as part of the "Great Society." During his presidency Johnson improved health care and education, worked to alleviate poverty and homelessness, and championed civil rights. Over 200 acts were passed, including the Wilderness Protection Act which saved millions of acres of forests, Elementary and Secondary Education Acts, Voting Rights Acts, Medicare, Immigration Acts, and many other acts aimed at alleviating troubling social conditions.

175) A bill must be passed by both the Senate and House of Representatives to become law. Who is able to break a tie in the Senate's vote?

A) No one, the vote must be taken again after further deliberation
B) President
C) Speaker of the House
D) Secretary of State
E) Vice President

The correct answer is E:) Vice President. The Vice President is also considered to be the President of the Senate. He does not have a vote, however, unless there is a 50-50 tie in the vote.

176) Which Act signed by President Andrew Jackson resulted in the Trail of Tears?

A) Native American Lands Act
B) Western Migration Act
C) Removal Act
D) Relocation Act
E) None of the above

The correct answer is C:) Removal Act. In the 1930s, Andrew Jackson signed into law the Removal Act. Tribes were forced to sign agreements which would allow the military and citizens of the southern states to "help" them relocate west of the Mississippi river.

177) In the majority of English-speaking countries anthropology has been traditionally studied within four related fields of study, what are those fields?

A) Biological, linguistics, psychology and sociology
B) Biological, socio-cultural, linguistic, and archeology
C) Socio-cultural, sociology, psychology, and economics
D) Linguistics, psychology, sociology, and sociolinguistics
E) Social psychology, psychology, sociology, and archeology

The correct answer is B:) Biological, socio-cultural, linguistic, and archeology.

178) This field of anthropology seeks to understand the physical human being through the study of genetics, inherited and the variations, evolution and adapta- tion. Which field of anthropology does this describe?

A) Anthopometrics
B) Socio-cultural anthropology
C) Biological (physical anthropology)
D) Forensic anthropology
E) Linguistic anthropology

The correct answer is C:) Biological (physical anthropology).

179) Prior to the Age of Exploration, the spice trade was primarily dominated by

A) Native Americans
B) France
C) Britain
D) Muslim merchants
E) Russia

The correct answer is D:) Muslim merchants. There was only one land route in existence and in addition to being treacherous, it was heavily controlled by Muslim merchants seeking to make their own profits on the spice trade. The high tariffs encouraged European rulers to spend great efforts in seeking another route to India and this spurred the Age of Exploration.

180) When Christopher Columbus set sail in 1492 he was looking for

A) A new land to claim in the name of Queen Isabella of Spain
B) Exotic food and gifts he could return to the people of Spain
C) A new route to India and easier access to valuable spices
D) Freedom from religious oppression he had faced his whole life
E) None of the above

The correct answer is C:) A new route to India and easier access to valuable spices. The high tariffs of Muslim merchants urged European rulers to spend great efforts in seeking another route to India. As a result, Christopher Columbus sailed across the ocean looking for an "Eastern Passage" and instead discovered the American continent. Frustrated by his failure to find passage to Asia, Columbus still called the native peoples "Indians."

181) Native American shamans are believed to gain information by

    A) Interacting with the spirit world
    B) Communications with tribal leaders
    C) Personal intuition and morality
    D) Information-gathering visits to other tribes
    E) Meaningful dreams and divine right

The correct answer is A:) Interacting with the spirit world. Shamans are believed to be deeply spiritual individuals who have access to the spirit world. Through meditation, chanting, fasting, drumming, and other techniques, Shamans are able to communicate with spirits (both good and bad) and receive information and help in knowing how to heal and help those in the natural world.

182) The US Open Door Policy involved

    A) An agreement that government information should remain open to the public
    B) Agreements between France and England to leave doors open for peace talks with the United States
    C) Cuban merchants being willing to trade with both Russia and the United States
    D) Fair and equal trade with China
    E) Both C and D

The correct answer is D:) Fair and equal trade with China. Despite earlier agreements of free trade in Asia, many European countries had begun establishing spheres of influence where they held powerful trade advantages in China. Fearing the disadvantage that this could bring, Secretary of State John Hay took action by circulating "Open Door Notes." His actions led to the Open Door Policy which allowed China to maintain its sovereignty and brought fair trade among nations.

183) Based on the theory of Divine Right of Kings, the king is believed to be responsible to and ultimately answer to

    A) Their subjects
    B) Their local ecclesiastical rulers
    C) Other monarchs
    D) God
    E) None of the above

The correct answer is D:) God. Divine Right is a belief that the right of the king to rule is given directly by God. As a result they both speak for God, and answer to no one but Him.

184) Which of the following is an ascribed status?

A) Nurse
B) Teacher
C) Doctor
D) Female
E) None of the above

The correct answer is D:) Female. An ascribed status is a status that an individual doesn't have any control over. For example, race, ethnicity, and gender.

185) The Equal Rights Amendment advocated

A) Gender equality
B) Racial equality
C) Religious freedoms
D) Ethnic tolerance
E) Opposition to age discrimination

The correct answer is A:) Gender equality. The matter of gender equality in the United States has been a popular topic of feminists throughout the 1900s. An Equal Rights Amendment which would constitutionally mandate that there could be no discrimination on a basis of gender was first proposed in 1923. By the 1960s, a strong push by feminist groups to get the amendment passed brought a new wave of support. However, due primarily to opposition by Phyllis Schlafly, the amendment failed.

186) Authoritarian governments are largely characterized by

A) Representation of the people
B) Centralized power
C) Individual rights
D) Dispersion of power
E) Both A and C

The correct answer is B:) Centralized power. Authoritarian governments are essentially the opposite of democratic governments. They tend to have a stronger focus on the centralization of power. The rights and powers of individuals are largely overlooked. Examples of authoritarian governments include totalitarian regimes, military governments, socialist governments, and monarchies.

187) Which of the following BEST describes role conflict?

A) A person in a play must do a role in which a person has conflicting emotions.
B) A mother feels obligated to both clean the house and cook dinner, but won't have time for both.
C) A person has two work projects which must be finished, but they will only have time to do one.
D) A person is told that they must finish a project at work, but to do so they will have to miss their child's soccer game.
E) None of the above

The correct answer is D:) A person is told that they must finish a project at work, but to do so they will have to miss their child's soccer game. Role conflict involves conflict between two different social roles. In this case, the role of a parent and an employee are in conflict.

188) The main problem with the Keynesian economic theory is

A) It incorrectly asserts that people will spend a lot of money during recessions
B) The assumption that foreign governments will be willing to purchase U.S. products at a premium
C) It requires creating a budget surplus to pay down any debts incurred once the recession ends
D) Its requirement that the government not increase spending until the recession ends
E) That it overlooks the effects of stock markets in leading to most recessions

The correct answer C:) It requires creating a budget surplus to pay down any debts incurred once the recession ends. The Keynesian theory is that governments should create deficits to spur the failing economy. This means that afterwards a surplus must be created by increasing taxes and decreasing spending - both of which are politically unfavorable actions.

189) Spartan government can be most accurately described as

   A) Authoritarian
   B) Democratic
   C) Theocratic
   D) Prosperous
   E) Authentic

The correct answer is A:) Authoritarian. Citizens of Sparta were sharply divided in class roles. Men, women, and a class of slaves were separated and trained in their specific roles. The city-state was ruled by two kings and a group of elders who made all decisions. In contrast to the democratic society of Athens, Spartan government was highly militaristic and authoritarian.

190) Which empire prevented Rome from expanding further east?

   A) Babylonian
   B) Parthian
   C) Greek
   D) Kurdistan
   E) Roman

The correct answer is B:) Parthian. The Parthian empire was a similarly powerful and formidable opponent and became an effective barrier to Roman expansion in the East. Although as emperor Trajan was able to conquer a small amount of Parthian territory, for the most part Rome was never successful in wholly defeating the Parthians.

191) The primary reason the Great Wall of China was built was to

   A) Protect against invasion by nomadic barbarians
   B) Stand as a symbol of the powerful Qin Dynasty
   C) Provide work for millions of destitute farmers
   D) Allow for more efficient communications by merchants
   E) None of the above

The correct answer is A:) Protect against invasion by nomadic barbarians. The Chinese empire had recently been established, and the great wall was an attempt to protect against invasions from barbarians in the north. It is still the most extensive defensive fortification ever built.

192) What was the central argument of the Zenger trial?

A) Taxation without representation is not valid or constitutional
B) Equal rights do not require that individuals use the same facilities
C) The Supreme Court does not have the power to issue a writ of mandamus
D) A person cannot be convicted of libel if their statements are true
E) Unconstitutional laws do not have to be upheld by the public

The correct answer is D:) A person cannot be convicted of libel if their statements are true. In Europe during the colonial period, individuals were convicted if they were found to have published statements critical to government officials. In the Zenger trial, however, Alexander Hamilton made the argument that a statement was libelous only if it were false.

193) Which of the following correctly lists the four Asian Tigers?

A) China, Japan, Nepal, and South Korea
B) Taiwan, South Korea, Japan, and Thailand
C) Hong Kong, Singapore, South Korea, and Taiwan
D) Japan, Singapore, Taiwan, and Thailand
E) China, Nepal, Taiwan, and Singapore

The correct answer is C:) Hong Kong, Singapore, South Korea, and Taiwan. The economies of these four countries grew exponentially between the 1960s and 1990s earning them this nickname.

194) In this field of applied psychology how our cognitive and psychological processes affect our interaction with tools and objects in the environment is studied. What field of applied psychology does this portray?

A) Human factors psychology
B) Industrial and organizational psychology
C) Educational psychology
D) Clinical psychology
E) Health psychology

The correct answer is A:) Human factors psychology.

195) The Imam Mahdi are to the Shiites as _____ is to Christians.

   A) Mary's virgin birth
   B) Christ's divinity
   C) The Holy Ghost
   D) Christ's Second Coming
   E) None of the above

The correct answer is D:) Christ's Second Coming.

196) In this geographical technique geographers group geographical knowledge into categories that can be explored globally. What geographical technique does this explain?

   A) Geographic information systems
   B) Systematic
   C) Regional
   D) Descriptive
   E) Analytical

The correct answer is B:) Systematic.

197) Geography can be divided into two main branches that can also be divided into a number of sub-fields. What are the names of the two main branches?

   A) Regional geography and geomatics
   B) Physical geography and human geography
   C) Environmental geography and human geography
   D) Human geography and regional geography
   E) Geomatics and environmental geography

The correct answer is B:) Physical geography and human geography.

Test Taking Strategies

Here are some test-taking strategies that are specific to this test and to other CLEP tests in general:
- Keep your eyes on the time. Pay attention to how much time you have left.
- Read the entire question and read all the answers. Many questions are not as hard to answer as they may seem. Sometimes, a difficult sounding question really only is asking you how to read an accompanying chart. Chart and graph questions are on most CLEP tests and should be an easy free point.
- If you don't know the answer immediately, the new computer-based testing lets you mark questions and come back to them later if you have time.
- Read the wording carefully. Some words can give you hints to the right answer. There are no exceptions to an answer when there are words in the question such as "always" "all" or "none." If one of the answer choices includes most or some of the right answers, but not all, then that is not the answer. Here is an example:

    The primary colors include all of the following:
    A) Red, Yellow, Blue, Green
    B) Red, Green, Yellow
    C) Red, Orange, Yellow
    D) Red, Yellow, Blue
    E) None of the above

    Although item A includes all the right answers, it also includes an incorrect answer, making it incorrect. If you didn't read it carefully, were in a hurry, or didn't know the material well, you might fall for this.
- Make a guess on a question that you do not know the answer to. There is no enalty for an incorrect answer. Eliminate the answer choices that you know are incorrect. For example, this will let your guess be a 1 in 3 chance instead.

 # What Your Score Means

Based on your score, you may, or may not, qualify for credit at your specific institution. At University of Phoenix, a score of 50 is passing for full credit. At Utah Valley State College, the score is unpublished, the school will accept credit on a case-by-case basis. Another school, Brigham Young University (BYU) does not accept CLEP credit. To find out what score you need for credit, you need to get that information from your school's website or academic advisor.

You can score between 20 and 80 on any CLEP test. Some exams include percentile ranks. Each correct answer is worth one point. You lose no points for unanswered or incorrect questions.

Test Preparation

How much you need to study depends on your knowledge of a subject area. If you are interested in literature, took it in school, or enjoy reading then your studying and preparation for the literature or humanities test will not need to be as intensive as someone who is new to literature.

This book is much different than the regular CLEP study guides. This book actually teaches you the information that you need to know to pass the test. If you are particularly interested in an area, or you want more information, do a quick search online. We've tried not to include too much depth in areas that are not as essential on the test. Everything in this book will be on the test. It is important to understand all major theories and concepts listed in the table of contents. It is also very important to know any bolded words.

Don't worry if you do not understand or know a lot about the area. With minimal study, you can complete and pass the test.

 Legal Note

All rights reserved. This Study Guide, Book and Flashcards are protected under US Copyright Law. No part of this book or study guide or flashcards may be reproduced, distributed or stored in a retrieval system, or transmitted in any form or by any means, electronic, mechanical, photocopying, recording, or otherwise, without the prior written permission of the publisher Breely, Crush & Associates LLC. This manual is not supported by or affiliated with the College Board, creators of the CLEP test. CLEP is a registered trademark of the College Entrance Examination Board, which does not endorse this book.

 References

[1] Young, Robert G., http://ryoung001.homestead.com/Freud.html Reprinted with permission.

FLASHCARDS

This section contains flashcards for you to use to further your understanding of the material and test yourself on important concepts, names or dates. Read the term or question then flip the page over to check the answer on the back. Keep in mind that this information may not be covered in the text of the study guide. Take your time to study the flashcards, you will need to know and understand these concepts to pass the test.

Monarchy	Democracy
Charisma	Federalist
Panama Canal shortened sailing time between which two American cities?	Green Revolution
Grapes of Wrath took place during which era	Anthropology

Governed by elected officials	Rule by kings and queens
Political party wanting a strong connection to the federal government	Magnetic personality
A time when there was a significant increase of agricultural products - 20th century	New York and San Francisco
The study of all human life aspects and culture	The Great Depression

Sociology	Muslim
Thomas Nast	Which method of data collection is the most comprehensive?
What type of data collection is done to track major demographics and population counts in the US?	How often does a Census take place?
Who said we have the right to "Life, liberty and the pursuit of happiness?"	What is the first amendment?

Contributed to the maths and metalwork	The study of human social relations and relationships
Face to face interview	Cartoonist for Harper's Weekly
Every ten years	Census
Church and State	John Locke

Who said "give me liberty or give me death"?	Mean
Mode	Median
Range	Earliest Human Innovation
Anarchy	Tyranny

Average	Patrick Henry
The middle number in a set of ordered numbers	The number that occurs the most often
Learning how to control and use fire	Difference between the highest and lowest numbers
A form of government with ruler that is a dictator	A state lawlessness and disorder

Oligarchy	Townsend Duties were placed on what items?
James Madison made which treaty?	What was the first nuclear powered submarine named?
Which President served a third term?	Law of Demand
Law of Supply	Conformity

Glass, lead, paint, paper and imported tea	A form of government where the power is in the hands of a few- sometimes elites and/or wealthy upper class
Nautilus	Treaty of Ghent
Where any given rise in the price of a product pulls down the quantity demanded	Franklin Delano Roosevelt
Consciously or sub-consciously keeping ones behavior pattern in line with that of the group	An increase in the price of any goods lead to a rise in the quantity supplied

www.ingramcontent.com/pod-product-compliance
Lightning Source LLC
Chambersburg PA
CBHW081828300426
44116CB00014B/2514